Typography pap

250101(00)
$46.00

Typography papers · 5 · 2003

Typography papers is published by the Department of Typography & Graphic Communication The University of Reading PO box 239, Reading RG6 6AU England

editor Paul Stiff

editorial group for this issue Katherine Gillieson, Eric Kindel, Robin Kinross, Paul Luna, Peggy Smith, Sue Walker

production manager Mick Stocks

Typeset in Monotype Ehrhardt and formatted in QuarkXPress at the Department of Typography & Graphic Communication, The University of Reading

Printed on Book Design Smooth, 120gsm² and printed and bound by Henry Ling Ltd, at The Dorset Press, Dorchester, England

Cover Sample letters from the broadsheet of A.J. Fullam's American Stencil Tool Works, 1865. See p. 83 of this volume.

ISBN 0 7049 1124 8

© 2003 *Typography papers* the authors and Department of Typography & Graphic Communication

Typography papers here returns for its fifth volume in seven years. There are several obstacles to our aim of appearing annually, so we ask for the continuing patience of our readers if we decide, for example, that it remains better to set off with our carriages full than to depart on time but half-empty.

Eric Kindel's recollection of stencil letters is the most thorough survey yet published of an often disconcerting category of letterforms in which, as he says, conventions of letter shaping may be wilfully disintegrated, disfigured, and abstracted. His copiously illustrated study is based upon careful observation of artefacts and also upon some judicious reconstruction work. For any future work on stencilled letters, Eric Kindel's paper will be the starting point.

Ole Lund traces a remarkable public debate about typography. It started in early 1959 – continuing for around two years – in response to the sets of letterforms designed by Jock Kinneir and Margaret Calvert for use within the sign system which they were designing for Britain's new motorways, and later its whole national road network. The argument was ostensibly about legibility and propriety, between the claims of capitals with serifs against sanserif small letters. Kinneir and Calvert's work pointed to the potential value of design in modern public life, and indeed the debate was about design as a visible form of social philosophy. Ole Lund's work in the archives brings the arguments to life and at the same time corrects some partial and misleading accounts already published.

In this issue we publish two accounts of design process, each providing rich insights into the context in which decisions get made – both at the drawing board or computer terminal, and also in the meetings room.

Edward Ragg questions Paul Luna about the designing of the Oxford Shakespeare within a crowding market for bardery. The roman style signals that this is not a book but a gathering of work which took shape as a group of separate editions. These included the *Complete works*, available in a single volume but offered in two formats and two orthographies.

John Morgan's documentary account of the designing of *Common worship* offers not only pictures of working papers from the design process (sketches, marked copy and proofs, trial settings, and forms – many of which can now be seen at the St Bride Printing Library, London) but also fifteen documents which suggest the lively and engaged character of the exchanges between designers, clients, and representative readers.

In a paper which is in part a reply to Alan May's in the first volume of *Typography papers*, Paul Shaw describes letters on fragments of what may have been a major public inscription of the Trajanic era. (They were discovered in Trajan's Forum, in the centre of Rome, just four years ago.) He argues, after close inspection of traces of surface working, that there is evidence here to support a method of making bronze inscriptional letters somewhat different to that proposed by Alan May.

PS, August 2003

Edward Ragg
and Paul Luna

Designing the Oxford Shakespeare: an interview with Paul Luna

The Oxford Shakespeare is the most authoritative, and radically revised, collection of Shakespeare's work. This interview charts the genesis of the first computer-generated Shakespeare and the design issues faced by Paul Luna and his colleagues at OUP. The texts discussed are:
William Shakespeare, *The complete works* (Oxford: Clarendon Press, 1986, large edn. released in both old- and modern-spelling versions) (figure 1)
William Shakespeare: a textual companion (Oxford: Clarendon Press, 1987)
William Shakespeare, *The complete works* (Oxford: Clarendon Press, 1988, compact edn. in modern spelling only) (figure 2)
All are under the general editorship of Stanley Wells and Gary Taylor, apart from *William Shakespeare: a textual companion* by Stanley Wells, Gary Taylor, John Jowett, and William Montgomery. Single editions of plays with individual editors are published in the Oxford World's Classics series under the general editorship of Stanley Wells. (figure 3)

The interview was conducted on 12 August 1999 at the Department of Typography & Graphic Communication, University of Reading, as part of research toward an MA dissertation in Publishing at Oxford Brookes University: Edward Ragg, 'Controversies of the iconic: the Oxford Shakespeare 1978–1987' (Shakespeare Institute Library, Stratford: catalogue no: q PR 3071).

author's address
Selwyn College
Cambridge
CB3 9DQ

epr21@cam.ac.uk

ER Were you employed as a designer at OUP prior to the Oxford Shakespeare or were you called in specifically for the project?

PL No, I was already at OUP. It had a centralized design department for all its academic and general books, and I was appointed senior typographer shortly after the point at which the project began to pick up steam. The first designer to work on the Shakespeare project was George Hammond who had joined from HMSO; he worked on it for about a year.

ER Was that prior to Stanley Wells's arrival?

PL No, that was after Stanley's appointment.

ER So at some point in 1978?

PL That's right. At that stage it was assumed somebody would be keyboarding the text on a conventional composition system. George had been preparing specifications for the printing division of OUP, when I took over. However, that more or less coincided with the decision to work from the tapes of Shakespeare plays that already existed in the university, and to process the text through a computerized typesetting system.[1] I took over the design at that point.

ER So what were the major differences between those systems and these tapes – the tapes that were used to construct Trevor Howard-Hill's concordance – how were these keyboarded?

PL I don't know. I assume they were keyed in by either research assistants or other people in the university. The university then had a centralized computing service which used to handle the bulk of the computer work. Obviously people then did not have PCs or Macs on their desks. So any computing they wanted to have done, whether it was on the scientific or the humanities sides, had to be done centrally.

ER When you began work on the project, how did you establish a design brief or working set of conventions? Did you draw on some of the previous attempts to construct an Oxford Shakespeare going back to R. B. McKerrow and Alice Walker, or were entirely new

1. For a more detailed history of the overall Oxford Shakespeare project and the setting of both old and modern spelling editions from the Howard-Hill tapes, see Edward Ragg, 'The Oxford Shakespeare re-visited: an interview with Professor Stanley Wells' *Analytical & Enumerative Bibliography* 12.2 November 2000 (Illinois: The Bibliographical Society of Northern Illinois, 2000), pp. 73–101.

Figure 1. The Oxford Shakespeare: *The complete works*, modern-spelling version. (*c.* 30 per cent linear)

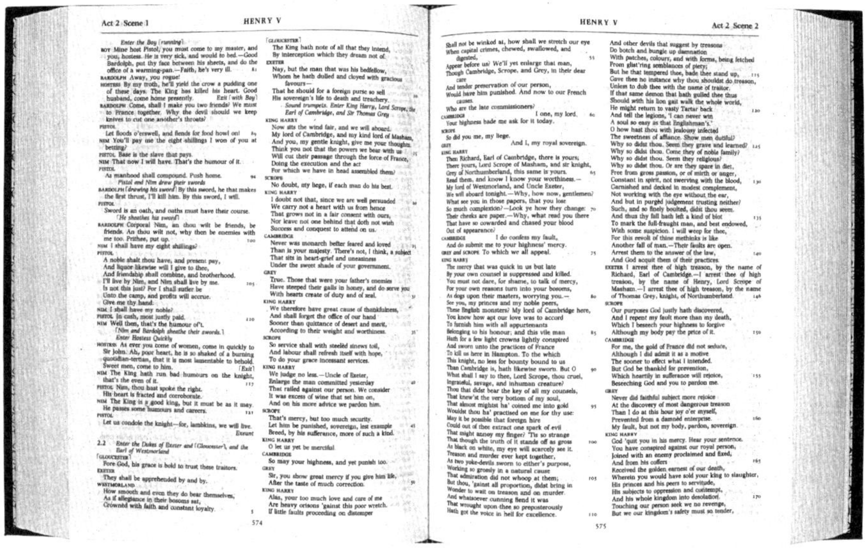

Figure 2. The Oxford Shakespeare: *The complete works*, compact edition. (*c.* 30 per cent linear)

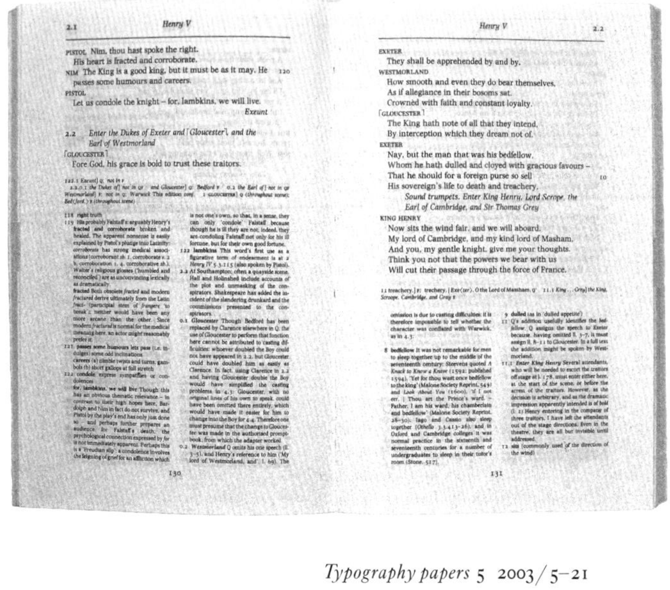

Figure 3. The Oxford Shakespeare: *Henry V*, paperback edition. (*c.* 30 per cent linear)

criteria involved? After all, this was, editorially speaking, supposed to be a very new, a very revisionist edition.

PL There were already plans for different editions which would involve different versions of the plays. But you have to understand the publishing background really. At that point there were two publishing businesses: there was the business in Oxford which published academic books and there was the business in London which published general trade books. There was the Clarendon Press in Oxford and the University Press in London. My arrival at OUP coincided with the gradual merger of those two businesses, the transfer of staff from London to Oxford and the beginnings of the merger of the academic and general trade publishing sides. One of the things that the trade publishing department expected was a compact, royal format, continuing-sale edition. For a long time that was called the *Oxford Standard Authors Shakespeare*.

ER So that was supposed to be the format for the Complete Works?

PL Yes, the *Complete works* in a single volume, that would be unannotated, and physically compact. The other editions they envisaged were a set of annotated single-play volumes. They were called the Oxford English Texts Shakespeare because they followed the editorial principles of the other OETs. OSAs had formerly been edited in London, but were then moved to Oxford; OETs were always edited in Oxford. So publishing precedent determined what the different departments wanted to get out of this project. The big volume *Complete works* was originally envisaged as the annotated edition with its major sale as a college text in the States. There was originally intended to be an annotated edition, both in a larger format and in royal OSA, an old-spelling edition, and an unannotated edition. Stanley Wells could probably confirm this.

ER Yes, he said that because the British tradition of producing Shakespeare single volumes of the *Complete works* involved unannotated editions, the idea was that OUP would surprise the British market by doing an annotated edition which could also be used to glean substantial American sales. But I'm not sure that both annotated and unannotated editions were envisaged.

PL Well, even the 'American college edition' ended up being unannotated.

ER Yes, because the Americans pulled out at the last minute, apparently on the grounds that there was a feeling that the Press would not be able to compete with *The Riverside*.[2]

PL Yes. We started designing a one-volume annotated edition that was very similar to the *Pelican Shakespeare*, designed by Hans Schmoller, with a similar format (figure 4).[3] The small format was, I think, royal (that's 234 × 156mm) and specimens were done for both. We certainly produced specimen pages trying out different styles of speech prefix, indent, and note sizes, to show the notes in one column and whether that was on the inside or the outside of the page. The single-play volumes were always going to be 216 × 138mm

2. *The Riverside Shakespeare* ed. G. Blakemore Evans (Boston: Houghton Mifflin, 1974)
3. *Complete Pelican Shakespeare* ed. Alfred Harbage (Harmondsworth: Penguin, 1969, 1981) 3 vols.

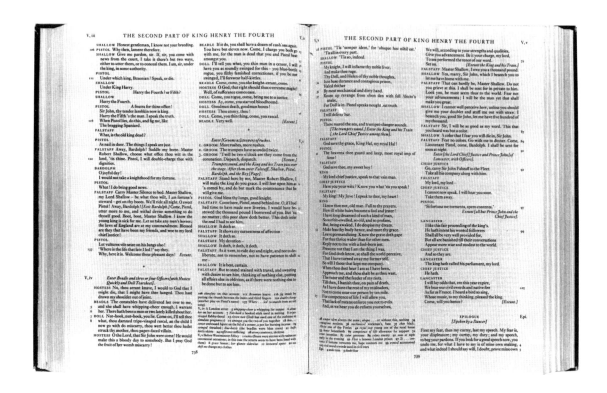

Figure 4. Double-page opening of
The Complete Pelican Shakespeare.
(53 per cent linear)

because that was the standard format of the OET series. These were
envisaged as single-column, with multiple banks of annotations:
collations explaining textual variations together with the more
general commentary. Those single-play editions were the ones
that changed least in their design concept, although they did have
to come into line with the typographic design of the two *Complete
works* editions because we were trying to design those at the same
time. Also we were trying to design the things in the abstract; none
of the texts had been edited. In fact many of the OETs still haven't
been edited. So we were working with sample material that Stanley
and Gary Taylor passed on to us – Gary was very much the engine
of ideas and Stanley directed the way it would be played.

ER   You've mentioned the influence of the *Pelican Shakespeare* and
Schmoller's typography. I was wondering whether the *New
Penguin Shakespeare* texts, those single-play editions, whether you
ever considered adopting their practice of putting the notes at the
back which can be an aid for some readers. Was there ever the idea
of adapting the OET design in that way?[4]

PL   No, I don't recall that. There was never any attempt to make the
OETs less academic. They were always the flagship of literary scholarship at OUP. They were supposed to announce their scholarship
and they do. If you look at Gary Taylor's *Henry V* there are many
pages on which there are only a few lines of text at the top of the
page and the rest of the page is taken up with annotation (figure 5).

4. The New Penguin Shakespeare series,
general ed. T. J. B. Spencer, associate ed.
Stanley Wells (Harmondsworth: Penguin)

ER   Wouldn't that, though, be something of a problem for designers? It
might look scholarly but it is in fact quite a hindrance to the reader.

Figure 5. Page from *Henry V*, paperback edition, showing minimum amount of text and maximum amount of annotation. (40 per cent linear)

It's certainly a frequent problem in the layout of, say, the *Arden Shakespeare*.[5]

PL Well, it was quite difficult to make up that volume. I checked all the proofs for it and was responsible for how the text and notes fit on the page. It had such a large ratio of notes to text that you had to make quite a lot of adjustments at proof stage to get things to work. But it wasn't just the scholarly material that proved complex. By today's standards the actual process of getting to see how things would look was frightfully protracted. We did specimens, we drew specifications, we marked up copy and then gave everything to the in-house typesetter who typeset them, output them to film, made ozalid proofs and only then could we look at the results. We eventually did all of this on our in-house typesetting system, but the OETs were always typeset outside.

ER Why was that?

PL It was to separate the OET work from the work on the OSA edition because the OETs had outside editors. Although Gary Taylor did edit *Henry V* most of the OETs were done by outside editors who prepared their own texts and notes – in those days people weren't using word processors, they were just preparing typescript. So the OETs were set from typescript rather than being processed on the text system.

ER So when it came to establishing a design brief, what kind of specimen did you set up? Presumably it was a piece with stage directions, act divisions and so on? I would be interested to know if you worked with a particular play.

PL We used *A midsummer night's dream* because it shows all the normal elements: it has songs and a play-within-a-play.

ER Yes, that's the play they chose as sample for the *Pelican Shakespeare*.

PL However, there was a lot of uncertainty about the final size of the Complete Works. The decision to do it with the final trimsize was taken quite late in the day. The idea was to be big, to appeal to the US market. I don't think anybody took on board the fact that it was going to be that thick. I do remember the absolute horror in the sales department when we had these bulking dummies made up and said 'This is the book you're going to get in the format you have all agreed'! Both Barry Townsend, the production director, and myself thought it was a bit over the top.

ER In that it would be too long and too bulky?

PL Yes, it's just too big, which makes it a desk book; it has to sit on a table. It's not really a portable book. But the pressure seemed to be from the US office: American college textbooks were large format. I think that what you report Stanley Wells as saying is correct. The Press wanted to make a splash, to make a statement that here was an Oxford Shakespeare. I'm sure that's why it must have been so large. But I felt that when the decision was made nobody had

5. The Arden Shakespeare Series, general ed. Richard Proudfoot (Walton-on-Thames: Nelson)

actually sat down and worked out how bulky and frankly how unwieldy an object it would be.

ER What is the actual format of that first hardback?

PL It's a format that we could print at the American printers. It's 279 × 216 mm.

ER And how does that compare with the smaller, compact version of the *Complete works* that appeared in 1988?

PL That was printed in the UK. That's 234 × 172 mm. The original format was somewhere between those two. It was 246 × 189 mm, which is a standard UK trimsize. That's what we would have worked from.

ER So you were working to a format that was not used for either of these two published editions?

PL Yes, for a long time we worked to a format that was between those two.

ER Was it solely a result of marketing and the American market that the larger, unwieldy format was adopted?

PL Yes. I must say that the original design was closer to the 1986 *Complete works* than the 1988 compact edition. The 1988 *Complete works* involves the compromises of a compact version. The layout in the 1986 edition, however, represents Stanley's ideal of a page. For example, the compactness of the 1988 edition results in line numbers being put in the text, which is less satisfactory than in the margins (figure 6). You can't always number the fifth line because the numbering is within the measure, if the line length is too long. But when you have a marginal system there are no constraints.

ER Is it just with verse lines, then, that you have this problem and not prose passages which could be tracked differently?

PL Well, you have got a problem with prose. More often than not you

Figure 6. Comparison of type size, measure, leading, and line-numbering from the 1986 edition (left) and 1988 compact edition.

---

of it. If I do it, let the audience look to their eyes. I will move stones. I will condole, in some measure. To the rest.—Yet my chief humour is for a tyrant. I could play
25 'erc'les rarely, or a part to tear a cat in, to make all split.
        The raging rocks
        And shivering shocks
        Shall break the locks
30   Of prison gates,
        And Phibus' car
        Shall shine from far
        And make and mar
        The foolish Fates.
35 This was lofty. Now name the rest of the players.— This is 'erc'les' vein, a tyrant's vein. A lover is more condoling.
QUINCE Francis Flute, the bellows-mender?
FLUTE Here, Peter Quince.
40 QUINCE Flute, you must take Thisbe on you.

QUINCE A lover, that kills himself most gallant for love.
BOTTOM That will ask some tears in the true performing of it. If I do it, let the audience look to their eyes. I will move stones. I will condole, in some measure. To the rest.—Yet my chief humour is for a tyrant. I could play 'erc'les rarely, or a part to tear a cat in, to make all split.   26
        The raging rocks
        And shivering shocks
        Shall break the locks
           Of prison gates,   30
        And Phibus' car
        Shall shine from far
        And make and mar
        The foolish Fates.
This was lofty. Now name the rest of the players.— This is 'erc'les' vein, a tyrant's vein. A lover is more condoling.   37
QUINCE Francis Flute, the bellows-mender?
FLUTE Here, Peter Quince.
QUINCE Flute, you must take Thisbe on you.   40

can only fit your line numbering into the last line of the paragraph. We wrote a routine that stated 'If you can't number line 5, then number line 6'.

ER So that was one of the regrettable design aspects to the compact edition?

PL Yes. I think that the page size is certainly better in the 1986 edition. We did experiment with photographic reductions for the 1988 compact, but they didn't look right. The type was just too small in relation to the competition.

ER Yes, *The Riverside* is fairly large by contrast in terms of type size.

PL Yes, that's the one set in Janson, isn't it? We did look at *The Riverside* – we had all these volumes in the office of course. *The Riverside* was the kind of touchstone, I think, particularly for the US side. They would say '*The Riverside* has this feature, so why can't we do the same?' You can see its influence in having half-tones in the text. They never reproduced that well. They are informative, I suppose, but I think that there we were pretty much driven by what other people had done, not in the way we designed it but in the elements we had to use in the design. I think we drove a nice line with the actual page design.

ER I was wondering whether there were any markedly contrasting design factors when it came to preparing both an old-spelling edition and a modern-spelling edition?

PL We had to prepare extra characters for the old-spelling edition because the typeface we were using was Photina. The original designs were done in Ehrhardt, George Hammond's specification. But when Richard Russell, who was the Assistant Printer, saw the designs in Ehrhardt, he suggested that he'd like to set some pages in Plantin. In the end we didn't use either typeface, we used Photina, partly because it drives a line down the middle of those two typefaces. It's more even than Ehrhardt, its thicks and thins are less exaggerated, but it's not quite as heavy as Plantin.

Another reason for using Photina was it was a relatively new typeface. Oxford put it in immediately after it was released by Monotype. We set quite a number of books in it and it hadn't been installed by many other printers. So while it wasn't an exclusive typeface, it still had some cachet. It was a slightly unusual choice. It also has some very good features: it's got very small capital letters in relation to its lower case, so where you've got a lot of verse, the capitals don't create a separate vertical line at the left of the column. The italics are even in slope. Photina also works very well in small sizes and we knew that we were going to have to set the annotation in the OETs at 7pt (figure 7). We knew that the range of point sizes was going to be between 7pt and 10pt, so we had to choose a typeface that would be right for that. Also, because Photina was one of the first typefaces for photo-typesetting, the actual fitting of the characters is really much tighter than many other faces, so it's very compact.

11 **sworn brothers** 'companions in arms who took an oath according to the rules of chivalry to share each other's good and bad fortunes' (*OED*). At 3.2.43. they are called sworn brothers in filching'; but that later qualified phrase does not justify the common interpretation of this unqualified one as 'brotherhood of thieves'.

Figure 7. Monotype Photina, 7/8 pt.

EHRHARDT PHOTINA

Figure 8. Comparison of Photina and Ehrhardt small capitals (24 pt).

BOYET: What then, do you see?
ROSALINE: Ay, our way to be gone.
BOYET: You are too hard for me.
Exeunt.

III. 1

Enter Braggart and Boy.
Song.
BRAGGART: Warble child, make passionate my sense of hearing.
BOY: Concolinel.
BRAGGART: Sweet air, go tenderness of years: take this key, give enlargement to the swain, bring him festinately hither: I must employ him in a letter to my Love.

LUCETTA
Ay, madam, you may say what sights you see;
I see things too, although you judge I wink.
JULIA
Come, come, will't please you go?   *Exeunt* 140

Enter Antonio and Panthino   I.3
ANTONIO
Tell me, Panthino, what sad talk was that
Wherewith my brother held you in the cloister?
PANTHINO
'Twas of his nephew Proteus, your son.
ANTONIO
Why, what of him?

And wilt not come? Come, recreant; come, thou child,   410
I'll whip thee with a rod. He is defiled
That draws a sword on thee.
DEMETRIUS ⌜shifting place⌝   Yea, art thou there?
ROBIN ⌜shifting place⌝
Follow my voice; we'll try no manhood here.   *Exeunt*

⌜*Enter Lysander*⌝   3.3
LYSANDER
He goes before me, and still dares me on;
When I come where he calls, then he is gone.
The villain is much lighter heeled than I;
I followed fast, but faster he did fly,
That fallen am I in dark uneven way,   5
And here will rest me.

Figure 9. Comparison of scene divisions from the Penguin Shakespeare *Love's labour's lost*; New Penguin Shakespeare *Two gentlemen of Verona*; Oxford Shakespeare *Complete works*. (67 per cent linear)

ER So there weren't many problems with kerning, then?

PL No, the character fit is very good. We used the fonts without any kerning pairs. Photina also has these loosely fitted, quite broad figures which in normal book work would be a problem because they stand out from the text, but for Shakespeare are ideal because there are never any figures in the text and you really want nice clear figures for line numbers and references. Photina also has excellent small capitals which we could use for speech prefixes. All the original designs had letter-spaced speech prefixes. But when it came to the pre-production, Ken Beckley, who was then a manager in the composition department at OUP, said 'If there's any way you can avoid letter-spacing those, it will save a lot of time'. You see, they couldn't automate the keyboard commands. They would have had to key any spacing that was different, and that value changed at the beginning and end of every speech prefix. So Ken said 'If you can design it without letter-spacing, we'd be awfully grateful'. Ehrhardt looks dreadful if you don't letter-space the small caps, but Photina's small caps are okay (figure 8).

ER So it really emerged as the ideal typeface for the project?

PL Yes, it had a lot going for it.

ER How symbiotic was your relationship with Stanley Wells in terms of the evolution of design? He described you as a very good and very accommodating colleague. What I'm getting at, I suppose, is what was the real driver, given that it is hard sometimes to distinguish between purely editorial and purely typographic features?

PL Well, there was some tension between Stanley's editorial principles and what OUP had been used to selling: very traditional-looking, compact single-volume editions with very clear act and scene divisions and tucked-in line-numbering, abbreviated speech prefixes, little differentiation between verse and prose, all the things that Schmoller had been looking at. This was what was expected by the people who were going out to sell these books. So there was a feeling that we were producing something that was a bit too academic, too far from the norm: for example, not having big act and scene divisions but making it look as if the whole play ran on. To be honest, as a designer, you did feel that your scope for doing something glamorous on the page was removed. There wasn't the opportunity to punctuate a page with a nice act-scene division, or use the space to group elements off and make them look more separate. So this very minimalist approach, just a line-space between various sections, did go against the grain. People felt it was a bit laid back. I think Stanley had quite a job to get across the idea that he was trying to present the flow of a performance, the fact that in Shakespeare's day there weren't these great big breaks between scenes in a stage performance, that the curtains didn't come down between the acts (figure 9).

ER Also I suppose one of the things the Oxford Shakespeare was radical in was redefining the actual positioning of some of those act and scene divisions as, for example, in the final act of *Macbeth*.

PL　And in *Pericles*, I think.

ER　Yes, well that was an entirely reconstructed text.

PL　Then there was the issue of the two versions of *Lear*. If you think of the book trade and the side of publishing that connects with the book trade: 'Two *Lear*s, Oxford must be mad!' But they got the coup of the new poem, 'Shall I die?'

ER　Yes, of course, Gary Taylor's discovery in 1985.

PL　But there were compromises. Stanley's single-page concise introductions to each of the plays were added at the last minute because Simon Wratten, the Sales and Marketing Director, said OUP could not publish a single-volume Shakespeare without plot synopses. Stanley Wells wrote them to fulfill that function.

ER　It's an odd decision though, even from a Sales perspective, because some people do not want to know the plot of a play before they read it. But to return to the actual production of the text, could you tell me more about the typesetting and proofreading parts of the projects?

PL　We had a central electronic database of the texts. OUP then bought a complete composition system based on the requirements of this project and the on-going requirements of other projects, particularly dictionaries. It was foreseen that there would be a need for in-house text editing and composition. (The Press thought that there was going to be more of this going on than actually happened in the end). Word-processors didn't exist then, or were more trouble than they were worth. So you had to have a computer system that could drive the typesetting system. There had been various experiments at OUP with doing text-setting on standard mainframe computers, on the computers that did the accounts and payroll and which could perform data-capture and receive typesetting commands. But the interface between the mainframe and the typesetting side, although it was done quite expertly – Richard Sabido, was manager for EDP and Ken Beckley on the film-set side – was quite a painful process because nothing was dedicated. Everything had to be written from scratch every time you wanted to do something.

　　In fact there was a period of experimentation with one of the very first IBM PCs. Jamie Mackay wrote routines that would number the lines and make the column breaks; and he wrote programs that effectively transformed the coding of the Howard-Hill tapes to provide a drive tape for the OUP film-setting department to send to the Lasercomp, to typeset the pages. Now he did do that. But whether it was because they projected the man-hours it was going to take across 38 plays and realized this was crazy, or whether the Press felt that it would be worth investing in a better system for the long-term, OUP then produced a tender-document and approached different suppliers to procure an editorial system that could cope with the amount of work. Basically, the Press were after something very similar to the systems that were then being installed by American metropolitan newspapers: where journalists could enter copy directly, subs could format text, operators could make up pages and the whole editorial process could be generally sped up. I recall that OUP went to Bedford Computing, to Miles 33, to Penta; and in the end it was Miles, based in Bracknell, that got the contract. They installed a Miles 300 system, later upgraded to a 400 system. This consisted of a central processing unit and what were called nodes, which were boxes of local processing units, and a number of dumb terminals: units with a screen and a keyboard but no hard-drives and no disk-drives. The hard-drives were down in the IT department along with the back-up drives and the main processing unit.

The whole system was a batch-processing system. So you would log on to your terminal, call up a file, it would eventually come up on your screen – this did in fact take time, because each terminal only had a little local memory – and so it would put just a small amount of text into your screen memory for you to work on. If you then wanted to do something to it, such as change all the spellings of 'labor' to 'labour', you would set up that command and you would have to go through quite a number of screens to do that, so it was quite command-intensive. If you put me in front of a Miles keyboard now I could still probably remember the key commands! Then you sent the file away, it went into a job queue and it would sit there for ages, you would go and do something else to another file and every now and again you would look at the job queue to see what had happened to the initial file. Eventually it would tell you that it was ready, that the processing had been done. It really was incredibly longwinded. This was fine if you were doing things where you knew what the result was going to be. But it was extremely frustrating if you were designing something and you wanted to see what it would look like. For example, if you thought 'If I put a bit more space between each of these paragraphs, what will that do to the number of pages?' you'd have to set it up, send it away and if there was another job going through, it could be hours until the file came back to you. If you do that now in Word, of course, it tells you the pagination immediately. That's certainly the way the editorial assistant, Christine, had to work: Gary would come along and say 'Change all *these* to *that* and all *those* to *that*' and the text would usually have to be modified overnight. You would come back in the morning hoping that there had not been an error – for example, an unexpected end of file – otherwise you'd have to do the whole thing again!

ER So this must have been a very laborious process, particularly when it came to producing old- and modern-spelling texts where you would have had to have had entirely separate files presumably?

PL I think I'm right in saying that the original texts were the old-spelling ones, weren't they?

ER Yes, they edited the plays in old-spelling first using the concordance tapes and then using a particular 'search and replace' program to modernize the spelling.

PL But the modern-spelling text was the first that went into production. We certainly started on that first.

ER But if the old-spelling texts were edited first, why weren't they the first to be composed?

PL Because I suspect that the old-spelling text wasn't publication-date-critical. The people who wanted it would wait for it. Certainly all the primary effort went into producing the modern-spelling *Complete works* for publishing reasons. Also the modern-spelling print quantity was much larger and it was printed in the States. The old-spelling *Complete works* was printed in the UK, which would have meant a shorter lead-time and no shipping time. If there had been a four-month print-bind-ship time for the modern-spelling *Complete works*, there might have been only a six-week print-bind time for the old-spelling *Complete works*. It could have finished two months later and still have been published at the same time. Everything had to be more planned then. Each play went round several rounds of proof. You didn't have laser printers printing everything out in the right typeface. You had generic printers with just one typeface which was distorted until it fitted the character widths of the typeface you were actually using. If a word was in italic it simply got slanted and if it was in bold it got struck twice!

ER So this is what hindered you in attempting to realize what the texts might eventually look like?

PL Yes, what you had to do then was to send a file away to the composition department and wait for a piece of bromide [photographic paper] which would look exactly like the page. The original idea was that we would proof everything on thermal printers (which were rather like fax machines, or halfway between a xerox machine and a fax machine). These proofers were cheap in relation to bromide, but because they were so smudgy and you couldn't write on them, if you xeroxed them they looked even worse. So toward the end of the project I think we just bit the bullet and paid for bromides because otherwise proof-reading for detail would have been very difficult. It's fine making your macro-level decisions, but after a couple of rounds of proof you've got beyond that, you are into fine tuning: 'Will that word fit on that line? If I were to hyphenate it there would I pull that bit back up?' You couldn't tell from the thermal proofs, but you could on the bromides. But the really clever bits were done by Jamie Mackay, the programmer, because the Miles system was nothing like Word or QuarkXPress. You didn't just click 'B' for bold and so on. Although there were commands that did everything, they were commands that were called by codes that you had to type in around the word you wanted in bold. For example, <cf3> meant 'this is a command, change the font to font 3 (which is bold)' and so on. If you wanted to put a special character in like a 'ct' ligature or something, you'd have to type the command for 'change font 11' and then '5', or whatever key had been assigned to that special character. So the actual keying-in of the commands was quite complex.

Many commands were converted from the code on the tapes which designated speech prefixes, prose lines, verse lines, unassimilated verse lines and so on. There was already a great document describing all the different elements. George Hammond started the design process and I completed designing a typographic format for every element in the book: a speech prefix, a speech prefix that was dubious, an exit stage-direction and entrance stage-direction and so on. All these had specifications. I couldn't key these into the system. Jamie had to write 'formats' for all the specifications, long strings of commands saying: 'change to small caps, change the point size, change the leading, do this, do that, flush it left, flush it right'. You got to know, for example, what the job format code was for an exit stage-direction. But otherwise the text was just littered with job format codes.

The other thing was that the Miles system was programmable to a degree that word processors simply aren't, even with macros. In other words, the line-numbering is handled by a routine which says: 'you will insert the line number, when the line number is five, if the space available for the line number is more than so many points, and if it isn't you number line six' and these were obviously very, very complicated. Plus the text for each play had to be processed overnight and it did take all night for this processing to take place. So in order to make the thing as flexible as possible, in case there was a change-of-mind about anything, the way Jamie wrote the routines was that he never made an 'absolute' command where he could set up a series of 'relative' commands. So he would say 'what you do *here* is based on the point size *there* and the measure *there* and the amount of space left *there*'. That was very computing intensive, because every time the system came to such a point it would have to look back and see what it had done in order to do the right thing. But you can imagine that that is, of course, enormously flexible, because all you need to do to change all those instances is to go back and change that one thing you did in the first place and that worked extremely well.

There was also a pagination routine. Once we had produced galleys to a constant number of lines, Christine Avern-Carr would go through them. Now you've got to have a logical end to a column. For example, you can't have the last line of a speech at the top of a page, or an entrance stage-direction at the foot. There are precise ways of deciding how you can break up text into columns. Though we tried to automate this to some degree, in the end we got Christine to go through manually doing all the marking up on equal-depth galleys. We agreed that there was a minimum and maximum number of lines that would fit into a column. We made the columns equal by ⅛ pt adjustment to the leading. So if the norm was 59 lines we could either have 58 lines or 60. The proviso was that if you have a 58 in one column you should try to avoid having 60 in the next column. That way we optimized the pagination of every play. We were already checking the line-ends and concluded that we would not let the text-system divide words in the text. I think there are some word-divisions which were manually inserted, but there are not very many of them. We did set the optimum standard word-space to produce even-looking pages and set minimum and maximum word space values.

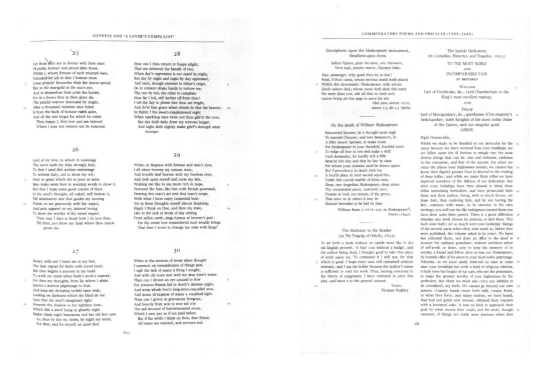

Figure 10. (left) Sonnets 27–30 from the 1986 edition. (40 per cent linear)

Figure 11. (right) Commendatory poems and prefaces from the 1986 edition. (40 per cent linear)

ER So how were those criteria modified for producing the sonnets or the non-dramatic verse? Was that generally less troublesome for the design?

PL Yes, but I don't think that the way the sonnets were laid out was quite ideal (figure 10).

ER I see there is a turned line in sonnet 32.

PL Yes. In retrospect I think I would have preferred to have kept constant alignments for the first line and the numbers, and let the sonnets hang with different amounts of space between them. In fact we set up a format that would justify each column vertically and put the line numbers in the right place by adding or reducing space at the points between the sonnets. But that was relatively easy. It was the 'Commendatory Poems & Prefaces' which involved more hard work.

ER Why did those take so long?

PL There are a large number of short items, and although everything else is so standardized, each one of these is quite different (figure 11). They contain odd things like centred lines, and it was a case of deciding how they were to be set. There must have been an editorial reason for the sequence of them. But it meant that to make the best fall on the page we had to decide what to take over or what to leave complete on any particular page. The text is obviously 'normal', but these pages required headings that do not exist in the plays. This is the sort of interactive design that the systems were least good at. It's easy to do on a desktop system, whereas we had to plan the whole thing in pencil layouts, key it in, see how it came out – whether it actually looked like the pencil layouts – and then, if it was wrong, it would be quite a tedious job to change it. Of course,

Come on, tune. If you can penetrate her with your
fingering, so; if none will do, let her remain; but I'll never give o'er. First, a very
excellent good-conceited thing; after, a wonderful sweet
air with admirable rich words to it; and then let her
consider.
⌐Music¬

⌐MUSICIAN¬ (*sings*)
Hark, hark, the lark at heaven gate sings,
    And Phoebus gins arise,
His steeds to water at those springs
    On chaliced flowers that lies,
And winking Mary-buds begin to ope their golden eyes;
With everything that pretty is, my lady sweet, arise,
    Arise, arise!

Come on, tune. If you can penetrate her with your
fingering, so; we'll try with tongue too. If none will
do, let her remain; but I'll never give o'er. First, a very
excellent good-conceited thing; after, a wonderful sweet
air with admirable rich words to it; and then let her
consider.
⌐Music¬
⌐MUSICIAN¬ (*sings*)
Hark, hark, the lark at heaven gate sings,
    And Phoebus arise,
His steeds to water at those springs
    On chaliced flowers that lies,
And winking Mary-buds begin to ope their golden eyes;
With everything that pretty is, my lady sweet, arise,
    Arise, arise!

Come on, tune. If you can penetrate her with your
fingering, so; we'll try with tongue too. If none will do,
let her remain; but I'll never give o'er. First, a very
excellent good-conceited thing; after, a wonderful
sweet air with admirable rich words to it; and then let
her consider.
⌐MUSICIAN ¬ (*sings*)
Hark, hark, the lark at heaven's gate sings,
    And Phoebus gins arise,
His steeds to water at those springs
    On chaliced flowers that lies,
And winking Mary-buds begin to ope their golden eyes;
With everything that pretty is, my lady sweet arise,
    Arise, arise!

Figure 12. *Cymbeline* 2.3.13–25.
Modern-spelling version, 1986 (top);
compact edition, 1988; single-volume, 1998. Note the original half-
brackets and the later, larger versions;
and the inconsistent justification of
lines. 16–18 in the single-volume
edition. (67 per cent linear)

when you're doing great reams of text the more automated, the more batch-orientated your system is the better it is because you don't have to change everything so frequently. And the commands for elements in the main text could be very complex. For example, with a three-part line, the lines have to overlap to fit the measure. So you would have three lines, one flushed left, one centred and one flushed right, but the overlap would have to be calculated and again Jamie would have written a routine for that. I suppose what I'm trying to emphasize is that each of these features didn't come as an off-the-shelf feature of the composition system. Instead you had to work out what you wanted to do and how to do it.

ER   So entirely new routines were having to be generated in order to carry out these design modifications?

PL   Yes, that's right. As I said, this programming was done by setting up various job formats which would call up a series of sub-routines. That's how it could be done effectively and efficiently. To avoid error the whole thing was broken down, as a programmer does, into step-by-step stages; and by making sure that you only define as much as you need to in each step. Then you just call up the next step to do the next bit of work. It did mean that Stanley Wells would say 'I want to have this looking like that', in general terms, and I would say 'That means we have to specify everything in terms of typeface, point size, spacing and so on'. Jamie would write the routines that would make that happen, and then Christine would key in that particular set of formats, and then we would go through the loop again.

ER   So there were several layers of consciousness as it were?

PL   Yes, exactly.

ER   So when you started to get through the programming and the type-setting phases and you actually started to get ozalids back, can you remember any particular modifications that had to be made at that stage or did the design start to appear as you had envisaged it?

PL   I think it did. I think we must have set at least a complete play in the subsequently abandoned smaller format before we proceeded. Most of the development was carried out in that format, then we went around and scaled everything up.

ER   So the change in format was in fact one of the major design changes, or at least resulted in a good deal of modifications?

PL   Yes. Another thing that we had to resolve was the fact that the line-ends of the large and small *Complete works* and the line-ends in the single-play volumes would all have to match (figure 12). Of course, this was difficult because the OET texts were edited separately so you have substantially different texts. But you have to get the designers to jump through some hoops, so we did the necessary calculations and we made sure that the point size-measure relationship was a constant across all editions and that all the indents related. Also, the word-spacing parameters were set in such a way that we could guarantee, as closely as one could, when things were being done in different composition systems: that speech in prose, for example, would line-break in the same way as on the Miles system in Oxford.

ER One thing that Professor Wells mentioned when I interviewed him was his regretting the use of broken brackets within the stage directions. Did that cause a design headache?

PL Yes. Again it was much less easy to produce special sorts in those days. You couldn't just do them in Fontographer. You had to decide what something would look like and then order it from Monotype, wait for it to be drawn and digitized, and if you didn't like it then you would have to pay for something else. That is, we prepared drawings to Monotype specifications, which they then amended and digitized. What I can't remember is what Stanley would have preferred instead of the broken brackets.

ER I think in retrospect that he just wanted to do the directions without the broken brackets because they were pretty confusing. It was found that they conflated the needs of the specialist reader and the general reader detrimentally.

PL Yes, I think that using angle brackets is more usual in a scholarly edition. Originally we intended producing half brackets that were more like quotation marks except with the vertical stroke lengthened.

ER Why were they felt to be better?

PL Well, we had looked at angle brackets, but I felt they looked really aggressive.

ER And they would presumably look quite dogmatic as well?

PL Yes. We had called them half brackets and it may have just come about as a result of a character on someone's keyboard in some system somewhere. I don't know. I do know that many square brackets, including Photina's, have horizontal bars that are too short and I prefer square brackets that have horizontal strokes that are elongated and slightly bolder. So broken brackets look like a kind of hockey stick, don't they? And the horizontal bars are slightly weightier. I don't think that in the end we were terribly happy with them, but they were required. I don't suppose that the average reader will understand why it's a half bracket as there aren't, as far as I can remember, any normal square brackets in the book. But I think that there was a desire to have something customized, or specific to the Oxford Shakespeare (figure 13).

ER It's certainly unseen in any other Shakespeare edition and I suppose, as well as the typeface chosen and the inconspicuous act and scene divisions, it was another way of signalling what was a very radical and rival edition.

PL Yes. The other special character we used was the little Tudor rose for certain act divisions. That was just an off-the-shelf Monotype special sort. That was used to indicate a stronger act/scene division than the normal blank line.

[Exit]
<Exit>
⟨Exit⟩
[Exit]
⌈Exit⌉

Figure 13. Comparison of brackets (from top): square brackets and angle brackets in the Monotype Photina Postscript font (top); narrow angle brackets from Linotype Mathe matical Pi font; square brackets from Monotype Imprint 'A'; and the special half brackets designed for the Oxford Shakespeare.

ER Were you still at OUP when it came to producing the compact
    edition?

PL Yes. It was like pouring water from one cup into another until it
    fitted! The good thing was by that time we had set the whole text
    and I was completely up to speed on what was in it. So it was simply
    a case of seeing if we could produce the thing. First we tried photo-
    graphic reductions of the full-size text. But there was still the idea
    of doing the book in royal and that would have been a huge reduc-
    tion. In fact the compact ended up in a wider format that Barry
    Townsend and I developed.

ER Even that makes the text pretty compact already.

PL But importantly it's still 234mm high. We argued that the important
    thing would be to rack it on the shelves with royal books. It would
    stick out but all that was needed was the right height. It is 16mm
    wider than a normal royal book but the same height. We needed the
    same measure relative to point size, of course, to retain the line-ends.
    So I calculated combinations of point size and measure that would
    generate the same lines. That's why the line numbers – although
    they are set within the column measure – are not allowed to push
    text on to the next line. They have to move rather than the text
    because that would change the line-ends.

ER And you would have had unsightly turned lines as well.

PL Yes. However, all of this effort does collapse if somebody says: 'The
    Oxford Shakespeare Romeo and Juliet act 1 scene 2 line 32' because
    you don't know whether that person is talking about all these con-
    sistent ones or whether they are talking about the separately edited
    OET text. There were other things that we changed in the compact
    though. We made the headline relatively more prominent. But the
    main difference is in the point size/line-feed ratio.

ER I suppose that was to maximize the usage of space whilst drawing
    attention to the title of each play.

PL Yes. If we'd simply photographed the 1986 *Complete works* it
    would be 200 pages longer than the compact and would have
    looked dreadful. So it was actually re-run. But all that needed to
    be re-run was the last stage really. The files that were used for the
    typesetting must have been duplicated, the formats were changed
    to move the line numbering and so on. Importantly, there's less
    leading relative to the 1986 *Complete works* but the formality of
    the structural element is the same. You still have the system of
    speech prefixes being set on separate lines for verse and on the
    same line for prose: visual things like that. But the headlines are
    bolder for quicker reference really. Most things were just re-
    specified to look the same though they were actually smaller.

ER You've mentioned that there are incongruities between the OET
    texts and the OSA *Complete works* editions. However, the Oxford
    Shakespeare has become something of a benchmark for
    Shakespeare design. I'm thinking particularly of S. J. M. Watson's
    comment that the Oxford Shakespeare 'may be said to have set the

6. S. J. M. Watson, 'Hans Schmoller and the design of the one-volume Pelican Shakespeare' *Typography Papers* 3, 1998, p. 133.

current standard for Shakespeare scholarship'.[6] Would you agree that the design developed here and educed from Schmoller's work has standardized design in producing Shakespeare editions?

PL Yes, we were looking at Schmoller's edition all the time. We would have done so anyway, because we knew it as designers. But, of course, there was Stanley Wells's connection with the Penguin. I remember sending out a page of the *Complete works* to Hans Schmoller asking for his comments. It came back with a comment to the effect that 'imitation is the sincerest form of flattery', which I was actually quite pleased with. You could have received a worse answer than that! He said we'd adopted practically all the things that he'd done in the Pelican. But there is the exception that Schmoller only numbered the lines he needed to number for that edition, that is for the notes, which is reasonable because you can still extrapolate other line numbers, although with slightly less ease, for any other line. But I think it's more sympathetic to generate them in 5s and 10s. In any case we never produced an annotated *Complete works*.

ER I'd like to ask you about the *Textual companion* and the compilation of that. Was that a complex part of the project to design?

PL No. It was relatively simple. We only did one layout for all the elements in a play because the book replicates the same design 38 times, or however many plays there are. We did need to look carefully at the make-up because of the multi-column settings. As for the diagrams and tables, as in the chronology and the summary of the control texts, we simply left space for those and they were then separately drawn and inserted. With the *Companion* everything that was conventional in the *Complete works* was retained and so it was relatively straightforward.

ER Finally, were there any other particularities to the design process which really aided the overall text's appearance?

PL I've mentioned the benefits of Photina. But it does have one flaw which we had to overcome: its punctuation is not particularly good. The commas are not distinguishable from the full points in small sizes and the same fault applies to the semi-colons and quotation marks. So we didn't use Photina's punctuation. Instead we used punctuation from Plantin, which is very clear indeed. I think this was originally done by Vivian Ridler and his designer Ken Stewart (figure 14). However, if you look very closely at some of the OETs you can see that Photina punctuation has been used instead of Plantin because different typesetters didn't follow the specifications accurately. But the *Complete works* volumes are consistent throughout.

'Hamlet, Prince of Denmark; Macbeth'
'Hamlet, Prince of Denmark; Macbeth'

Figure 14. Photina punctuation as designed (above) and as amended for the Oxford Shakespeare.

Paul Shaw

A recent discovery in Trajan's Forum:
some implications for understanding bronze inscriptional letters

In *Typography Papers* 1 (1996), Alan May explored several methods of infilling square-cut Roman inscriptions. This article draws on the recent discovery of an inscription in the Foro Traiano whose square-cut letters are outlined by a series of grooves. It challenges Alan May's conclusion, and instead postulates the use of a method involving metal pattern letters.

author's address
785 West End Avenue
New York, NY 10025
USA

paulshaw@aol.com

Preparations for the Grande Giubileo del 2000, Rome's celebration of the millennium, resulted not only in the cleaning and restoration of many monuments, churches, and palazzi, but also in new archeological discoveries. One such discovery, made by a team of archeologists headed by Professor Eugenio La Rocca, Sovraintendente ai Beni Culturali del Comune di Roma, coordinated by Dr Silvana Rizzo, and under the scientific direction of Dr Roberto Meneghini, was an inscription in three contiguous fragments found on 23 August 1999 in the southern portion of the Foro di Traiano where an arcaded piazza meets the northern portico of the Foro di Augusto. The fragments are part of a white lunense marble plinth or string-course that may have functioned as a parapet.[1]

The inscription is in the nominative:

[CAES]AR · NERVA · TRAI[ANO]

The break between the first and second fragments occurs in the middle of the N of NERVA while the break between the second and third fragments runs through the V. The first two fragments are side by side with the inscription facing up. The remaining fragment is lying on its side nearby with the inscription facing away (figures 1 and 2). The letters are square-cut and were originally filled with gilded bronze. There is still bronze (with a patch of gilding) intact for the interpoint between NERVA and TRAIANO and mortar or cement remains in the stem of the R and the bottom of the left stroke of the V in NERVA (figures 3 and 4). Tang holes are present for every letter. Stylistically they are reminiscent of those in the famous inscription at the base of Trajan's Column which is located at the northern end of the Foro Traiano.

Despite its brevity the inscription is of interest for several reasons. The first reason is the superficial similarity of these square-cut letters to the contemporaneous v cut letters of the Trajan inscription.[2]

1. 'The discovery in their place of three adjacent fragments of a continuous plinth of white Luna marble as wide as the string-course, and with the central part occupied by an inscription bearing the name of Trajan in the nominative, with letters 15 cm high, originally filled with gilded bronze, seems to suggest that this piece of work was intended to be placed between the two levels on the string course itself, or on an added masonry course in the manner of a parapet. The original length of the text (my thanks for this suggestion to Elisabetta Bianchi) was about eleven metres, much less therefore than the space available on the three porticoed sides which seems to have amounted to fifty metres. This suggests that the text might have been repeated several times, or that it has come down to us not only with some gaps, but also incomplete where the dedication is concerned. It is possible that in the missing part of the inscription there was some reference, which has so far escaped explanation, to the functions of this uncovered and almost inaccessible area.' (Meneghini 2001, p. 262) I would like to thank James Mosley for his help in smoothing out the rough spots in my translation.

2. Dr Roberto Meneghini has proposed that the fragmentary inscription can be dated to the final years of Trajan's life. (In an e-mail, 10 October 2002.)

Figure 1. The first two fragments of the inscription in the Foro Traiano discovered in 1999. (© 2003 Legacy of Letters Digital Photo Archive)

Figure 2. The third fragment of the 1999 Foro Traiano inscription.

Figure 3. Detail of A · TR from the 1999 Foro Traiano inscription; the interpoint is bronze infill with a patch of gold leaf in the middle.

Figure 4. Detail of RVA from the 1999 Foro Traiano inscription; note the cement or mortar in R.

Figure 5. Inscription (CIL Vi 920a) currently on a wall of the courtyard of the Museo Nuovo of the Palazzo dei Conservatori celebrating Claudius' victories in Britain (43 AD). See also figures 14 and 15.

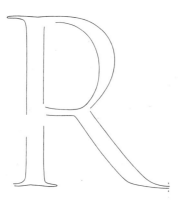

Figure 6. Tracing of R21 by Edward Catich from the Trajan Column inscription. (From Catich, 1961)

Second is the fact that these letters are lighter than other surviving examples of square-cut letters, like those in the fragmentary inscription celebrating Claudius' victories in Britain in 43 AD (figure 5) or on the Arch of Septimius Severus, 203 AD.[3] And third is the presence of evidence that may shed light on how bronze-infilled letters were made.

The letters of the Foro Traiano inscription range in height from 145 mm (E) to 160 mm (second A) and have stem thicknesses that vary from 20 mm (E) to 24 mm (second R). Their stem width to letter height ratio is roughly 1:7 in contrast to the 1:9 ratio that characterizes the letters of the Trajan Column inscription[4] (figure 6). The serifs are more heavily bracketed in the former than the latter. These differences undoubtedly reflect the contrasting methods of lettercutting of each inscription. There are other, subtler differences between the Foro Traiano capitals and those of the Trajan inscription. A has an inner serif on the right leg; the counter of R is more symmetrical and lacks a lower right 'corner'; the arms of the T are wide; and the interpoint is a triangle rather than a calligraphic stroke. Clearly the Foro Traiano letters were not made by a scriptor wielding a broad-edged brush in the manner proposed by Father Edward Catich in *The origin of the serif* (1968, 1991). And yet they are unmistakably imperial in style. Were they modelled on the letters of Trajan's Column?

It is not surprising that the letters of square-cut inscriptions tend to be noticeably bolder than those of v-cut inscriptions. The thin strokes must be heavier to accommodate the bronze infill. As a result the stroke contrast so characteristic of imperial capitals is reduced in square-cut inscriptions. For example many of the letters of the Claudian inscription at the Capitoline are nearly monoline. In contrast the letters of the Foro Traiano inscription have nearly the same 2:3 horizontal/vertical stroke ratio as that of the Trajan Column letters.[5] Their elegant appearance reflects the importance placed on an inscription destined for the largest and most ambitious of the Roman forums.

The surface of the plinth is smooth at the edges with a rough band in the middle framing the inscription. Richard Kindersley hypothesizes that the plinth was smoothed at the edges to make its ovolo moulding more visible from a distance. The middle section was left untouched since it was going to be filled with the inscription.[6] There are no visible guidelines for the inscription, but close examination of the rough surface reveals a series of four or five parallel grooves, spaced 2 mm apart, surrounding each letter and interpoint[7] (figures 7, 8, 9, 10). These grooves are clearly distinct from the surrounding surface. What was their purpose? They could not have had a decorative function since they are only visible at very close range. Instead they must have played a role in the formation of the inscription. That is, they were made before the letters were carved and infilled rather than after. They may be evidence for an alternative theory of how bronze infilled letters were produced to the one advocated by Alan May (1996).

3 CIL Vi 920a and CIL 6.1033 respectively.
4. Measurements of Trajan inscription based on Catich (1961); measurements of Foro Traiano inscription based on rubbings made by me 19 July 2002.
5. Proportions are 7:11 versus 13:20 for the E (upper arm) and 8:12 versus 16:23 for T.

6. E-mail 17 October 2002 from Kindersley, who viewed the fragmentary inscription with me on 20 September 2002.
7. The existence of the grooves was pointed out to me by Elisabetta Bianchi, assistant to Dr Meneghini, during my first visit to see the inscription on 19 July 2002. I do not know if other square-cut inscriptions have similar grooves, but those in the Roman Forum as well as on the Arches of Titus, Septimius Severus and Constantine have been so subjected to weathering and restoration that any grooves originally present are no longer visible.

Figure 7. Detail of RA from the 1999 Foro Traiano inscription; note the alignment and the series of grooves outlining both letters.

Figure 8. Rubbing of R2; note the series of grooved lines.

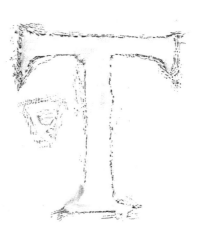

Figure 9. Rubbing of interpoint and T; note the series of grooved lines.

Figure 10. Rubbings of A1 and E; the lower left corner of the E is missing; note the series of grooved lines surrounding A1.

May, after testing out several possible methods, concluded that the most plausible one was as follows:

> Take separate casts of each of the letter cavities and the surrounding stone surface using either clay, softened wax, or plaster ... Make female impressions in sand, clay, or plaster of those parts of the casts that are below the original stone surface. These new 'moulds' are effectively duplicates of the original letter cavities. Cast bronze infills from these duplicate cavities. (May 1996, p.126)

This method assumes that the letters were first written on the surface according to the Catich manner and then carved in stone. Kindersley, a lettercutter with several decades of experience, is sceptical. 'Instinctively I feel the process of cutting the letters first, making a positive, then a negative for casting from is far too complicated and fraught with difficulties,' he writes. 'For example, the carved letters have straight vertical sides making it very difficult to remove a negative mould from the marble.' But the real sticking point for him is the problem of shrinkage of the bronze after casting.[8] May, who used lead instead of bronze for his experiments, suggested that cold-working of the cast letters after insertion into the cavities might have solved this problem, though Kindersley remains unconvinced. (May's solution requires that the letters be made of an alloy of bronze, tin, and lead to provide the proper malleability for cold-working).[9]

Kindersley and I, intrigued by the grooves of the Foro Traiano fragment, have postulated another method, one that avoids the shrinkage issue entirely. It assumes that the bronze letters are cast in sand moulds, with tangs intact, before the inscription is carved. A piece of timber whose thickness matches the length of the tangs is laid on the plinth and aligned with the bottom of the text. The bronze letters are then assembled along the length of the timber and the position of their tangs marked. Sockets for the tangs are cut and the letters are inserted into the stone so that they are flush to the surface. Next, outlines of the letters – the series of parallel grooves – are traced onto the stone and the letters removed. Using the outlines as a guide the inscription is cut vertically into the stone. Finally, the original cast bronze letters – along with some cement as a bonding agent – are inserted into the cavities.[10]

Not only does this theory account for the grooves but it also explains the lack of guidelines, the bulbous serifs and the misalignment of the letters. In outlining the letters multiple grooves are used to ensure that the outline is visible against the rough surface of the stone. The existence of a single outline for the ARN in CAESAR · NERVA – the serifs of the right leg of the A and the stem of the R are joined as is the leg of the R and the left serif of the N – supports the notion that the entire inscription was assembled at once rather than letter by letter (figures 1, 11, 12). The use of a piece of timber as a guide to arranging the letters would obviate the need for scratched guidelines of the kind often found on v-cut inscriptions. The misalignment of the letters – most noticeably the slight rightward tilt of the first A in TRAIANO and the E in NERVA – suggests that they shifted before being outlined (figure 7). (Once the bronze letters were inserted into the tang holes the timber would have been removed and thus there would have been no guide to insure perfect alignment). The bulbous serifs – as well as

8. In an e-mail, 18 November 2002, from Kindersley; he also stressed the problem of shrinkage in an e-mail of 17 October 2002.
9. May: 'If their bronze letters were cold-worked after casting, the bronze they used must have been a compromise alloy.' He suggests the addition of tin and lead (May 1996, p. 128).
10. In an e-mail of 18 November 2002 Kindersley solves the riddle of how to deal with the tangs, a problem that had me stumped when I first proposed this process to Richard: 'To answer the latter, the process would be to cast the letters off site in a foundry from sand moulds with the tangs intact. The tangs would be approximately 30mm long. A piece of timber 30mm thick would be attached to the marble aligning with the bottom line of the text. The letters with their projecting tangs would be set up in the timber and the tang position marked up onto the marble. Next the tang recesses would be sunk into the marble and the letters would then be placed flush in the sockets, the exact position refined and the outline traced back on to the marble for recessing to receive the casting.'

Figure 11. Rubbing of R1 and interpoint from the 1999 Foro Traiano inscription; note the join with the preceding A.

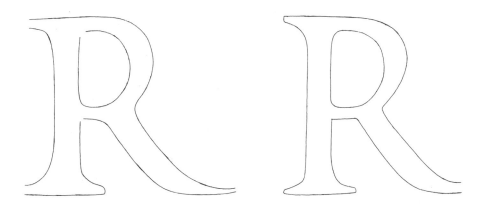

Figure 12. Outlines of R1 and R2 traced from rubbings to show the disparity between the two letters.

Figure 13. Repeat of figure 7, showing detail from the 1999 Foro Traiano inscription; see the alignment of R A and the series of grooves outlining both letters.

11. In an e-mail of 18 November 2002 from Kindersley: 'Interestingly all the serifs show a swelling (distortion) which could be due to the effect of shrinkage of the metal while cooling after casting.'

the soft junctures of strokes – reflect the fact that the letters were cast before they were carved.[11] Close inspection of the Claudian inscription reveals many of the same layout quirks as in the Foro Traiano fragment: inconsistent spacing, letters joined at the serif (e.g. EN and AT in SENATVS), tilted letters, and uneven alignment (figures 14, 15).

This method is essentially the same as that proposed by Susini in *The Roman stonecutter* (May's method C) in which letters cast from prepared patterns are used as models to cut the letters in the stone. Pointing out that the letters and tang hole positions of square-cut inscriptions are not identical for similar characters, May dismissed this theory. But his objection was based on the assumption that 'If such

Figure 14. Detail of the upper portion of the Claudian inscription at the Museo Nuovo of the Palazzo dei Conservatori. Note the raised C in line 1, the raised O in line 3 and the alignment of IM in line 4.

Figure 15. Detail of the lower portion of the Claudian inscription; note the alignment of IM on the bottom line, the dropped Q in the third line (as well as the differing sizes of the letters below its tail), the alignment of LA and IA and the dropped C in the second line, and the alignment and relative sizes of B and R in the top line.

a method had been used, we would expect to find that each of the occurrences of any letter of a particular size in an inscription would be identical, as it would not have been necessary to have more than one pattern for each character' (May 1996, p.126). This assumption may be logical, but not necessarily true. The three As, three Rs and two inter-points of the Foro Traiano inscription are all different, but that does not mean that they were not cast before being carved. Their bulbous serifs and curved stroke junctures are more typical of casting than of carving. Perhaps, despite the inefficiency, the Romans cast each letter of an inscription as needed.

Although circumstantial, the most telling evidence in favour of the notion that the metal letters were made first is the poor spacing of square-cut inscriptions. The letters, unlike those of v-cut inscriptions, tend to be positioned as closely together as possible, suggesting that they were physically assembled before being carved. This conclusion is reinforced by examples of letters that are misaligned and crooked (e.g. the MA in MAX of a square-cut inscription currently in the depository of the Foro Traiano, figures 16, 17) as well as some that may be upside down (e.g. several of the letters S in the inscription on the Arch of Septimius Severus). The overall impression of a square-cut inscription is of a group of disparate letters thrown together rather than of a rhythmic and harmonious whole.

This variation of the Susini method is based not only on the circum-stantial evidence of the letters comprising the Foro Traiano inscription but also, in Kindersley's words, 'on how we would tackle this problem today'. It has several advantages over May's preferred method. First of all it is simpler. Second, it avoids the problem of shrinkage in casting bronze letters. Third, it guarantees that the bronze letters will fit the carved cavities without any additional recourse to cold-working or other strategies. And lastly, it can be used to prepare inscriptions horizontally on the ground or vertically *in situ*. Of course, as May said, no method can be considered definitive – including this one – until we have more information on the surviving bronze letters themselves.

Figure 16. Inscription, discovered in the 1930s, in the depository of the Foro Traiano (underneath the Via Fori dei Imperiali). Note the tilted A and T on the second line.

Figure 17. Detail of the inscription shown in figure 1, showing parts of lines 1 and 2. Note the mis-aligned MA. (© 2003 Legacy of Letters Digital Photo Archive).

My thanks to Dr Roberto Meneghini and Elisabetta Bianchi for access to the inscription and additional assistance with the background of its discovery; to Garrett Boge for additional photographs and for making a full-scale rubbing of the inscription; and to Richard Kindersley for his valuable insights into the technical aspects of lettercarving.

references

Catich, Edward M. 1961. *Letters redrawn from the Trajan inscription in Rome*. Davenport, Iowa: Catfish Press, St Ambrose College

Catich, Edward M. 1991 (1968). *The origin of the serif: brush writing & roman letters*. 2nd edn (ed. Mary W. Gilroy). Davenport, Iowa: Catfish Press, St Ambrose University

Claridge, Amanda. 1998. *Rome: an Oxford archaeological guide*. Oxford and New York: Oxford University Press,

Limentani, Ida Calabi. 1991. *Epigrafia latina*. 4th edn. Bologna: Cisalpino Istituto Editoriale Universitario

May, Alan. 1996. 'Roman bronze inscriptional lettering: notes on methods of production'. *Typography papers* 1, pp. 123–29

Meneghini, Roberto. 2001. 'Il foro di Traiano: Ricostruzione architettonica e analisi strutturale'. *Mitteilungen des Deutschen Archäologischen Instituts Römische Abteilung* band 108, and *Bulletino dell'Istituto Archeologico Germanico Sezione Romana* vol. 108, pp. 245–68

John Morgan

An account of the making of
Common Worship: Services and Prayers for the Church of England

This paper, compiled from first-hand experience of the job, tells the story of the making of *Common Worship*. The design process is revealed in documents and artefacts pulled from the shallows of everyday exchanges between designers, clients, and readers. By 'thinking-out-loud' and placing design procedures in their normal context, this article aims to let the job speak for itself.

author's address
John Morgan studio
115 Bartholomew Road
London NW5 2BJ

john@morganstudio.co.uk

The 13th of September 2001 was announced by some English newspapers as a 'day of prayer' following the attack, two days earlier, on the twin towers of the World Trade Centre in New York. Prayer for many people on this day was implicit and perhaps even wordless. Every generation finds new ways to confront and express the feelings they have in common.

The forms of service and worship of the Church of England were theoretically fixed in *The Book of Common Prayer* (*BCP*, sometimes known as '1662'). 'Common' distinguishes the prayers gathered in this book from those said in private. However, liturgy continues to develop, and experimentation with new forms of service culminated in the *Alternative Service Book* of 1980 (*ASB*). With experience of its use, the weaknesses as well as the strengths of the *ASB* became apparent. Through its governing body the General Synod, the Church began to revise the *ASB*. The result was *Common Worship* – 'services which bring together the best of both ancient and modern, classic and contemporary'.[1] From 1 January 2001 the Church of England has had two sets of liturgies for worship: those in *The Book of Common Prayer* (which remains permanently authorized) and the new services in *Common Worship*.

The full title *Common Worship: Services and Prayers for the Church of England*, tells us this much: first, it is more than one main service book, it is a collection of resources published in books, booklets, cards, on computer disks and available free on the internet; second 'common prayer' (that is, shared forms of worship) expresses the unity in the wider Church of England while allowing for variety and local responsibility. *Common Worship* was designed to be used across the whole breadth of the Church of England.

The process of producing *Common Worship* was exhaustive and involved all parts of the church, starting with the Liturgical Commission, which produced the first drafts. These went to the House of Bishops, which amended the texts and sent them to the General Synod, where representatives of the clergy and laity, with the bishops, debated the drafts. 'Revision committees' then considered and amended the drafts in response to the debates in Synod. When revision was complete the House of Bishops again considered the texts. Finally the General Synod voted on the final form of the services. The authorization dates were set and the process of publication began.

In contrast to the *ASB* which was published by a consortium of publishers, *Common Worship* was published by Church House Publishing, the Church of England's in-house publisher. With the advantages of production under one roof and with no shareholders,

1. *New liturgy for the Church of England is coming soon*, Church House Publishing, 2000

prices were kept as low as possible (the standard edition was published at £15).

The *ASB* had already abandoned the official dress of the 'blue-book'[2] precedents of the privileged presses. It still however followed the traditional aesthetic of a dense full page – a survival from a time when paper was expensive and scarce. In terms of production *The Book of Common Prayer* may have reached its peak in 1760–3 when John Baskerville printed at Cambridge University Press using types and paper of his own design. But Baskerville's editions were the most expensive available and so were unable to compete against cheaper priced competitors. Baskerville's editions are still appreciated as monuments of printing for their typographical excellence. There are other models to look to, with less typographical ceremony. The very first, 1549, edition of *The Book of Common Prayer* was printed in black ink on cheap paper and at a cheap price.

More often though, it was on books of this kind that scribes, illuminators, and printers turned out their most decorated work. This led to a liturgical style so imposing that it has not been uncommon for new publications to reproduce not only the text but also the typography of an earlier edition. There is still a greater readiness to look at these books and manuscripts as examples of production, or for their strong appeal as 'typography', even though the text and typography are inseparable.

In this account I discuss the project from a purely typographical point of view.[3] It may be helpful to read the contents list of the standard pew book, which I refer to here as the 'standard edition'. It shows (figure 1) that the book includes both modern and traditional language and modern and traditional orders of service.

The design and production of *Common Worship* was notable in many ways, not only in the size of the task, the print-run (the total number so far produced of all editions, separate booklets, and cards amounts to 910,000) or in the noble heritage of precedents, but in the open, transparent nature of the production. Each stage from brief to book launch was clearly defined and managed. The openness to comment and criticism from clergy and laity was essential in achieving the widest assent possible. In this sense the making of *Common Worship* could be a model for certain kinds of book production in the future.

My intention is that the transparent nature of the job will be echoed in this account of production as it happened, without embellishment and with little commentary – using the key job documents,[4] letters and samples themselves or edited extracts from them. The documents are those sent and received by Omnific,[5] the appointed design group of *Common Worship*. The hope is that by exposing the process, the job should speak for itself.

It remains to be said that this kind of designing and making is collective work. In the absence of a full colophon within the printed books, this account goes some way towards acknowledging the many hands involved in the making of *Common Worship*.

2. Stanley Morison referred to the old official 'blue-book' style of the privileged presses: 'Its form marked it for what it was: a print annexed to a statute- or blue-book.' (Morison, Stanley, *English prayer books, an introduction to the literature of Christian public worship*, Cambridge, 1943) To clarify: *The Book of Common Prayer* was 'annexed to a statute' (the Act of Uniformity). The *ASB* was a collection of services authorized by the General Synod.

3. For an introductory outline to *Common Worship* see Bradshaw, P. (ed), *Companion to Common Worship*, volume 1, 2001.

4. Much of the daily correspondence and transfer of text between publisher and designers took place through e-mail (only a fraction of which is included here). The more informal and frequent nature of these exchanges contrasts greatly with the letters now lodged in the ASB job archive held at the St Bride Printing Library, London.

5. Omnific, a mainly editorial design studio, was founded in 1983 by Derek Birdsall RDI. During the production of *Common Worship*, Omnific was four people – Derek Birdsall, Shirley Birdsall, Elsa Birdsall and John Morgan.

Figure 1. Contents page from the
'standard edition' (the standard pew
book). The Holy Communion section
is printed in red, as are the running
feet in that section.

Note on the figures: the *Common
Worship* editions were printed in black
and red. Red reproduces as grey
within these illustrations.

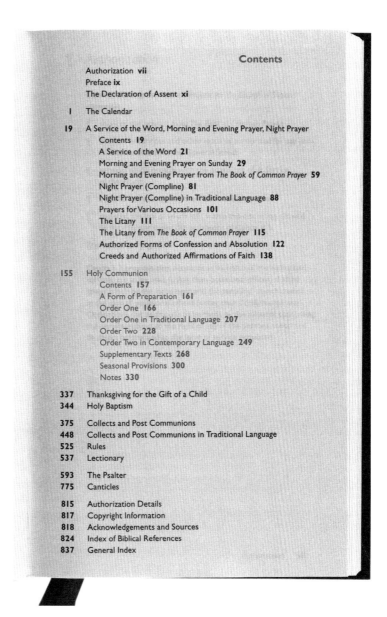

Figure 2. The groups and sub-groups
behind *Common Worship*.

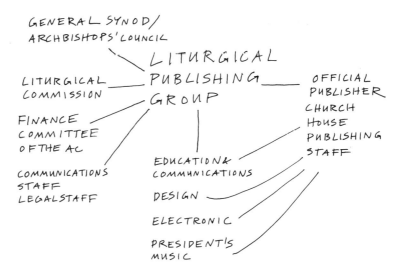

A Liturgical Publishing Group had been set up to oversee the publishing process. This in turn established a Design Panel to select the designers and approve the design for *Common Worship*.* On 21 July 1999 a design brief and project description was sent out by Dr Colin Podmore, Secretary of the Liturgical Publishing Group, to eighteen potential designers (document 1). Eight designers or design groups expressed interest in the project, and on the basis of their letters and examples of their previous work, three were short-listed: Et Al, Graphic Thought Facility, and Omnific.

* Members of the Panel were: Professor Christopher Frayling, Rector of the Royal College of Art; Alison Baverstock, publisher, marketing consultant and author; Canon Jeremy Haselock, Precentor of Norwich Cathedral, member of the Liturgical Commission; Dr Colin Podmore, Secretary of the Liturgical Publishing Group; Rachel Boulding, Liturgy Editor, Church House Publishing; The Revd Dr William Beaver, Director of Communications of the Church of England.

DOCUMENT 1   1 September 1999

The Design Project

· The Church of England is preparing a new series of worship books under the title *Common Worship: Services and Prayers for the Church of England*. The main volume in the series will be a book containing the Sunday services, and will be published in November 2000. At the same time various offprint booklets and cards, as well as parallel electronic products, will be issued. From 2001–2005 a short series of further books will be published using a similar design as part of a 'family of volumes' containing all the main services.

· The new books will bring together traditional and modern elements in worship of the Church, and thus heal divisions between old and new. They will be inclusive of different styles and approaches.

· The Church is looking for a design of the highest quality, which will unify the publications and provide a strong visual identity across the text and covers of the materials.

· Over a million people attend Church of England churches each week in every town and village in England; most of them will soon be using the new books. The publications will therefore be very significant in the life of the Church and of the country as a whole. A sample copy will be presented to the Queen in November 2000 and events are planned in cathedrals throughout the country to celebrate the publication.

· The market is people who go to church – both regular attenders, who will use the books every week, and occasional visitors, who might come for baptisms, weddings or funerals. Individuals will buy the books and churches will order them in bulk. The books need to have a layout clear enough to be easy to follow at a glance – classic, but visually interesting.

The Task

· As the project is so important in the life of the Church, the decisions taken about it need to enjoy the widest assent possible.

A large number of (often conflicting) interests have to be satisfied. One of the main qualifications for the chosen designer or design group will therefore be a willingness and ability to work with the Liturgical Publishing Group (the committee, made up of clergy, publishers, administrators and others, given the job of overseeing the publication) and to be flexible in responding to its concerns.

· The chosen designer or design group will also need to work closely with the publisher, Church House Publishing (an in-house body) and its staff.

The Design Brief

Principles

A number of considerations will need to be borne in mind in the design:

· *Use* – The Common Worship books will need to be designed for **use**, as well as for appearance. They will be held up and read aloud from in church, as well as being used by individuals at home, so they must be clear and straightforward to read. In this way, they are different from most other books.

· *Excellence* – The books must give an impression of excellence and quality. The worship of God deserves the best that we can offer. Furthermore, they will be used in most of the Church of England's parishes and so will be a flagship project for the Church – they must do it credit.

· *Long term Value* – The design must be one of lasting quality and appeal, such that it will still give a positive impression in twenty years' time.

The Identity, Image and Style of the Church of England

The worship of the Church of England is an expression of its identity. In publishing its new services, the Church will be signalling what it stands for. It is the Established Church and has a duty to offer pastoral care to all. It ministers in diverse social contexts with differing needs, from cathedrals to inner city estates. The visual style towards which the Church (through its new Archbishops' Council) is working is one of understated elegance and quality, of a church which is both reassuring and challenging. The tone of voice which all communications need to reflect is calm and confident.

A Classic Look
The new worship materials are likely to be in use for at least twenty years, if not more. Many people hope that they will mark the beginning of a period of stability, after much change. So it is important that the design should not look dated in a few years' time. However, just as it should not be tied to the present, it should also not be locked in the past. It deals with the worship of God, who is eternal. The design should therefore have a certain timelessness about it – a look which is classic but not old-fashioned.

Disability Issues
The design will need to bear in mind at every relevant point the needs of members of the Church of England who are partially sighted, are colour blind, or have problems with manual dexterity. This is not to say that these needs will necessarily be fully met. Compromise will be required. At each relevant point the designer will need to address various needs and consider how far these can met. For example, with regard to the needs of the partially sighted, the Royal National Institute for the Blind's *Clear Print Guidelines* should be taken in consideration and the RNIB will continue to be consulted during the development of the design.

Further Details
Some further details might be helpful in order to fill in some background.
· *Typeface and Font size*
Readability and elegance of appearance are essential. The needs of the partially sighted and the fact that the books will often be used in conditions of poor lighting will need to be borne in mind.

• *Colour of Spoken Text and Instructions*

There is a need to distinguish clearly between spoken text and service instructions. It is anticipated that this will be done by the use of two colours and possibly by further design features (red italics have been used elsewhere for this purpose – the traditional use of red gives rise to the term 'rubric'). Again, readability is an important consideration, both by the partially sighted and the colour blind.

• *Distinctions within the Material*

The books will contain the following different types of material, each of which needs to be clearly distinguishable:

– different levels of headings;

– material which must be included in a service and material which can be left out;

– text to be said by the minister and text to be said by the congregation (the latter is customarily printed in bold type);

– choices between alternative texts, where it is intended to give steer towards one as being more generally preferred;

– notes.

With all of this, clarity and readability are of prime importance.

• *Leading and Margins*

The layout needs to be spacious and never cramped, but not extravagant. There needs to be sufficient margin so that the text does not disappear into the gutter when the book is lying flat.

• *Line breaks and Page turns*

These will need to be checked to ensure that they are acceptable. (For example, there should not be a page-turn during the middle of a prayer.)

• *Dimensions*

The format of the books is important. There is pressure for the main pew book not to be too thick (both to assist those with manual dexterity problems and to preserve elegance). At the same time, the pages should not be too large because the book needs to sit happily on pew ledges both when closed and when opened flat. The pew book will be published in at least one other format.

DOCUMENT 2   20 September 1999

Extract of a letter from Dr Colin Podmore to Omnific

We would like to invite you to meet us and give a brief presentation at 10.15 am on Wednesday 13 October in the Jerusalem Chamber of Westminster Abbey (directions enclosed). The presentation should last for no more than 5–10 minutes, and would be followed by an interview of 20–25 minutes.

As a basis for discussion, please would you produce a sample page design of the three double-page spreads on the enclosed disk, in the format of the main volume, using two colours. We would like to see the samples before the meeting and so would you send them in by 4pm on Thursday 7 October.

The tight deadline is a reflection of the urgency of the project. The selected designer or design group would be expected to work between October and May, with a particularly intense period in the initial stage, up until mid-December.

The designers who are not selected will be paid a release of £250. Payment to the chosen designer will be made on a fixed-fee basis, though the overall budget is limited. You are asked to give some consideration to this in preparation for the interview.

I am also enclosing for information the full text of the Holy Communion services, from which the three double-page spreads for the design sample are taken.

Request for Design Sample

We would like you to produce a sample design of three double-page spreads of extracts from the Holy Communion service for the Standard Edition.

Format: 185 × 124 mm. Two colour printing.

The enclosed disk contains the texts, saved in Word, WordPerfect and rtf formats.

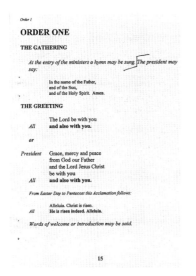
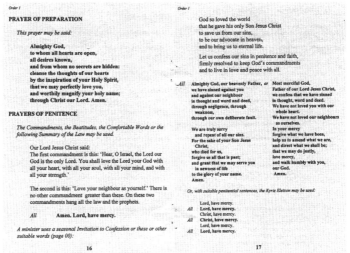

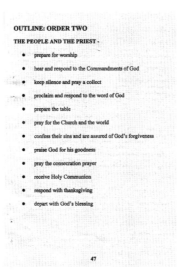

Figure 3. Page spreads from the Holy Communion booklet as supplied (photocopied black onto pink paper) 210 × 150 mm.

Figure 4. Pencil sketch by Derek Birdsall, September 1999. A first response to the Holy Communion booklet (figure 3). His notes indicate the intention to employ a 5 mm grid and to range headings right.

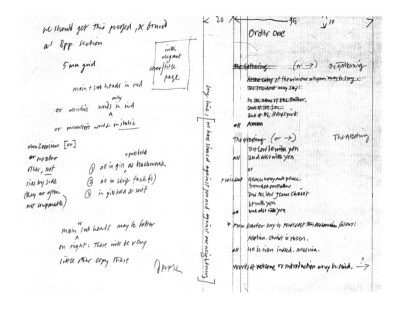

Figure 5. Ink-jet printed hand-bound 'Chinese-fold' booklet, one presented to each member of the Design Panel ; page size 185 × 124 mm.

The rubrics were returned to their traditional colour. The blue rubrics in the *ASB* were referred to by some as 'Blubrics'. Appropriately enough, given *Common Worship*'s place in the tradition of English liturgical books, 'Sarum red' (Pantone 485) was eventually chosen as the second colour. ('Sarum red' is from the Use of Sarum (Salisbury), the version of the Latin liturgy which was most widely used in England before the Reformation.)

The headings were ranged right (later to be refined). The liturgy is provided with clear signposts; if all the headings had ranged left, the text would have appeared to be one long stream. Ranging the headings right, as Birdsall argued, makes each a distinct 'label' above the 'cloud' of each prayer: 'You can read and understand the structure of the page with your eye corners.'

Setting alternative prayers in two columns, and reducing the type size to fit, was undesirable (see figure 3), although more economical. Better to run one prayer after the other ensuring that the page turn does not fall between them and that they are contained within a spread.

The 'outline order' shows the first introduction of the pilcrow (¶) as a more appropriate alternative to the ubiquitous 'bullet point' of office documents (see figure 3). Concerns were initially expressed that computer users would assume it to be an 'invisible' paragraph mark; but the pilcrow has a traditional use within prayer books to signal the beginning of new paragraphs or sections.

The booklet is shown at actual size on the opposite page.

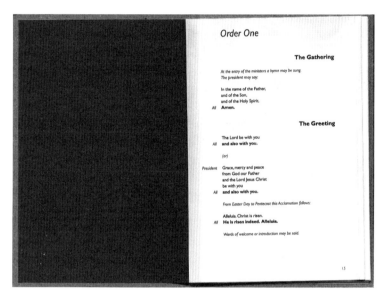

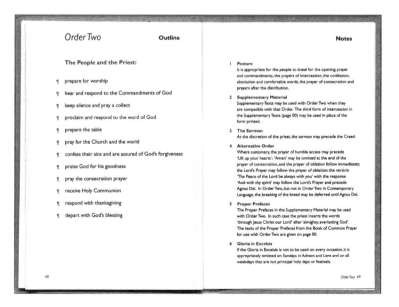

Let us confess our sins in penitence and faith,
firmly resolved to keep God's commandments
and to live in love and peace with all.

All   **Almighty God, our heavenly Father,**
       we have sinned against you
       and against our neighbour
       in thought, word and deed,
       through negligence, through weakness,
       through our own deliberate fault.

       We are truly sorry and repent of all our sins.
       For the sake of your Son Jesus Christ,
       who died for us,
       forgive us all that is past;
       and grant that we may serve you in newness of life
       to the glory of your name.
       Amen.

(or)

       Most merciful God,
       Father of our Lord Jesus Christ,
       we confess that we have sinned
       in thought and word and deed.
       We have not loved you with our whole heart.
       We have not loved our neighbours as ourselves.
       In your mercy
       forgive what we have been,
       help us to amend what we are,
       and direct what we shall be;
       that we may do justly,
       love mercy,
       and walk humbly with you,
       our God.
       Amen.

Prayer of Preparation

This prayer may be said:

All   **Almighty God,**
       to whom all hearts are open,
       all desires known,
       and from whom no secrets are hidden:
       cleanse the thoughts of our hearts
       by the inspiration of your Holy Spirit,
       that we may perfectly love you,
       and worthily magnify your holy name;
       through Christ our Lord. Amen.

Prayers of Penitence

The Commandments, the Beatitudes, the Comfortable Words
or the following Summary of the Law may be used.

Our Lord Jesus Christ said:
The first commandment is this:
'Hear, O Israel, the Lord our God is the only Lord.
You shall love the Lord your God with all your heart,
with all your soul, with all your mind, and with all your strength.'

The second is this: 'Love your neighbour as yourself.'
There is no other commandment greater than these.
On these two commandments hang all the law and the prophets.

All   **Amen. Lord, have mercy.**

A minister uses a seasonal Invitation to Confession
or these or other suitable words (page 00):

God so loved the world
that he gave his only Son Jesus Christ
to save us from our sins,
to be our advocate in heaven,
and to bring us to eternal life.

16

Omnific's direct response to the request for the design sample is shown in figures 4, 5, and 6. An inkjet-printed, hand-bound, Chinese-fold booklet was handed to each member of the Design Panel along with the trials and the note shown as document 3.

Note from Omnific made to accompany the initial layout

Common Worship

Approach

Comfort, clarity and poetry are the guiding principles. Particular attention has been paid to the hierarchy and disposition of headings, to line breaks in both the prayers and instruction, and to the inter-linear spacing and pauses.

Typeface

Our research and trial proofs to date indicate Gill Sans as the clearest typeface, partly because albeit a sanserif, it was designed in the humanist tradition; each weight, and particularly the italic is a text face in its own right.

Whilst the use of sanserif may be surprising, I am confident that clarity will swiftly achieve familiarity.

Layout

In bookwork, the best layouts appear to have designed themselves: e.g. pp. 20–21 in our layout. To achieve this it is necessary to scan the copy back and forth, evaluating the options, rather than simply 'pouring' the text in. The very nature of this text will particularly require and repay this attention.

Format

If economically possible a slightly longer page (say plus 10mm, or 185mm high) may be more balanced in the hand and allow longer passages to be elegantly contained on a page or spread, and may save pages in the long run.

Figure 6. Somewhat half-hearted trials of typefaces other than Gill Sans were made (Joanna is shown here). In the designers' minds it was always going to be Gill Sans. Omnific recognized that the recommendation of a sanserif might be controversial – though hardly shock of the new, Gill Sans now being over seventy years old. There was no strong competition from a more contemporary English sanserif. Much of the text needs to be in bold, and Omnific found almost every seriffed bold to be unsatisfactory.

An envelope was submitted to the design panel containing early trial proofs and alternative layouts. Omnific was the only design group to show rough work. The panel remarked on how helpful these roughs were in giving a useful insight into the final choice of design.

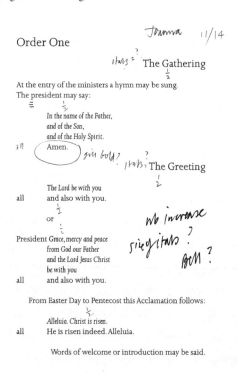

Though the essential elements of the design would remain consistent with the initial presentation, a later rationale submitted by Ominfic to Church House Publishing elaborates on the choice of typeface and format (document 4).

6. The version used was Adobe's 'Monotype Gill Sans'.

7. The standard edition was enlarged to 124 per cent for the desk editions, resulting in a format of 250 × 155 mm (1:618). For the President's edition the grid was enlarged to 147 per cent, with wider margins added so as to facilitate opening and reading on a lectern; the resulting format was conveniently 297 × 210 mm (A4).

8. A fundamental principle in the design of *Common Worship* is the avoidance of page-breaks (even across a spread) in the middle of prayers. Wherever possible, each prayer is complete on a single page, and rather than 'pouring the text in', if the space at the foot of a page is insufficient for the next prayer, it is simply left blank and the next prayer begins at the top of the next page. This approach sounds obvious but may not conform to a publisher's idea of harmony and economy (e.g. a balanced double spread of full and equal text columns). This not only avoids the rustle of pages turning during a prayer; it also contributes to clarity and gives a relaxed and comfortable appearance.

As Brooke Crutchley explains, some of the tricks in page layout are more subtle: 'All Cambridge editions of the Book of Common Prayer made sure that the Communion of the Sick finished at the foot of a right hand-hand page, so that the eye would not be caught by the heading of the service which, logically if unhappily, immediately followed – the Burial of the Dead. But neither the Oxford nor the Queen's Printer showed the same delicacy.' (Crutchley, Brooke, *To be a printer*, 1980: The Bodley Head, London, p.162)

9. Crutchley reports that when Cambridge University Press were invited to submit designs for the Series 3 Order for Holy Communion (the forerunner of the *ASB* service) 'We introduced a novel feature in the use of blue for the rubrics, instead of the traditional red, which tends to dominate the text.' The Liturgical Commission did not favour the proposals, however Crutchley continues 'it is satisfactory to note that the typography of the eventual *Alternative Service Book* bears more resemblance to our setting of the Series 3 Communion than to that of the published version.' (Crutchley, Brooke, *To be a printer*, 1980: The Bodley Head, London, p.167)

10. To prevent paper dust 'picking off' a 95 per cent tint of red was used rather than a full solid.

DOCUMENT 4   October 1999

Derek Birdsall's note accompanying Omnific's submission to the Church of England

Typeface

It is appropriate to use an English type design and obvious candidates were the types of Eric Gill, namely Joanna, Perpetua and Gill Sans. Trial pages were prepared in these types together with Univers, Bell and News Gothic.

As a clear distinction was required between the words spoken by the priest, the congregation, and from the instructions, the ideal typeface would have equally clear distinction between the Roman, bold and italic. Early research and trial proofs showed Gill Sans[6] to be by far the clearest: this is partly because it is designed on humanist lines (particularly the rather cursive italic) and because there is the clearest distinction between roman, italic and bold; indeed they are distinct but obviously related typefaces. (There is an additional light version which is useful for alternative versions of prayer and for 'running feet'). In a book of some 900 pages distinct folios are vital and consequently are in bold. After identifying the most typical longest lines, 9 point was chosen which seems to be best when 'leaded' 3 points.

Page size and format

A page of 186 by 124 mm had been proposed. However, on identifying the typical longest prayers e.g. the Creed, it became evident that to break the least number of prayers a deeper page size of 202 mm would be ideal. To rationalise this decision further a page format of 202 by 125 mm performs a 'Golden rectangle' i.e. a proportion of 1 to 1.618. This produces a book which is comfortable in the hand, creates the least possible number of interruptions in the prayers and fits in the pocket or handbag.[7]

Layout

The principle of avoiding breaks in prayers is followed generally throughout the layout,[8] resulting in a relaxed and comfortable appearance. To avoid the names of prayers or parts of a service becoming mere sub-headings, these are ranged right in bold 11pt, giving them far more distinction and incidently ranging on the 'backed up' (left) margin. Instructions are both in italic (for the colour-blind) and in the traditional red. To compensate for these appearing slightly smaller than the black roman type, the size of the italic is 9.1 point. A larger red italic (15 point) is used together with the traditional paragraph sign ¶ to signal sections. The word 'all' in red italic, is set out distinctively in the left hand margin opposite any bold i.e. congregation text.

Paper and colour[9]

Ivory paper gives the pages a warmer appearance, blends the red and black gracefully and reduces show-through on the 55 gsm weight. Solid red pages[10] are used to signal major sectional breaks and red running-feet and folios are used throughout the Holy Communion section.

Cover

The coincidence of *Common Worship* being two words of almost identical length, placed across the vertical sub-title *Services and Prayers for the Church of England* at the word *Church* produces an elegant solution to what could have been the trickiest design problem of them all.

Figure 7. The *ASB* designed in 1980 by Keith Murgatroyd. The cover is festooned with calligraphy in stark contrast to its plain interior. The *Common Worship* title is given visual form on Derek Birdsall's cover design.

Figure 8. The 5 mm grid and type sizes used in the standard edition. Meaningful white space follows silence for reflection.

			13mm								
			The Beatitudes ◄— 11pt				**Confession**			
			◄— 12pt line space							
			Let us hear our Lord's blessing on those who follow him. ◄— 9pt/12pt		All	Father eternal, giver of light and grace, ◄———— 9pt/12pt			
						we have sinned against you and against our neighbour,			
			Blessed are the poor in spirit,			in what we have thought,			
			for theirs is the kingdom of heaven.			in what we have said and done,			
					◄— 6pt half line space	through ignorance, through weakness,			
			Blessed are those who mourn,			through our own deliberate fault.			
			for they shall be comforted.			We have wounded your love			
						and marred your image in us.			
			Blessed are the meek,			We are sorry and ashamed			
			for they shall inherit the earth.			and repent of all our sins.			
						For the sake of your Son Jesus Christ,			
			Blessed are those who hunger and thirst after righteousness,			who died for us,			
			for they shall be satisfied.			forgive us all that is past			
						and lead us out from darkness			
			Blessed are the merciful,			to walk as children of light.			
			for they shall obtain mercy.			Amen.			
			Blessed are the pure in heart,			*Or another authorized confession may be used.* ◄———— 9.1pt/12pt			
			for they shall see God.						
						Absolution			
			Blessed are the peacemakers,						
			for they shall be called children of God.			Almighty God, our heavenly Father,			
						who in his great mercy			
			Blessed are those who suffer persecution for righteousness' sake,			has promised forgiveness of sins			
			for theirs is the kingdom of heaven.			to all those who with heartfelt repentance and true faith			
						turn to him:			
						have mercy on *you*;			
			Silence for Reflection			pardon and deliver *you* from all *your* sins;			
						confirm and strengthen *you* in all goodness;			
						and bring *you* to everlasting life;			
						through Jesus Christ our Lord.			
					All	**Amen.**			
10mm	10mm	5mm	75mm	15mm	10mm	10mm	10mm	5mm	75mm	15mm	10mm
	164	*Holy Communion*	20mm						*A Form of Preparation*	**165**	

The *ASB* was produced in 1980 before the advent of desktop publishing and the Macintosh computer. In *Common Worship* the roles of designer and typesetter were one and the same. By typesetting the text themselves the designers were able to find pragmatic configurations beyond the reach of the traditional drawing-board designer. The next stage involved producing a template and style sheets in QuarkXpress. A grid was made from 5 mm intervals (see figure 8).

DOCUMENT 5   25 October 1999

Letter from Rachel Boulding[11] to Omnific

There will be plenty to discuss, setting a larger number of pages should raise quite a few questions. We would also like to go over the following areas, as by that stage we should all have a clearer idea of where we are:
· any questions about the design itself;
· the contract (by that date we should have sent you a draft to consider);
· the logistics of how we work together;
· modifications to the draft schedule;
· how we handle disability questions, including the RNIB Clear Print Guidelines;
· plans for marketing materials using the elements of the design;
· how we deal with the music.

In the mean time, I enclose print outs and disks of the following material:
· the revised version of the Holy Communion service – this is a later version of the pink booklet sent to you earlier (for example, the All instruction in the margins have been taken out – clearly we'll need to talk about this);
· the Lord's Prayer text, to be inserted on pages 24 and 70 in parallel columns;
· two pages of music (see letter from Alistair Warwick which explains the technical details);
· our liturgical House Style Guide

DOCUMENT 6   8 November 1999

Announcement of Designers for Common Worship

1. I am delighted to be able to report that the LPG's Design Sub-Group has, with the approval of the Bishops of Guildford and Salisbury, selected Derek Birdsall RDI and John Morgan as the designers for *Common Worship*.[12]
2. The announcement was made this morning at a press conference held in the Senior Common Room of the Royal College of Art (RCA) by Prof. Christopher Frayling, Rector of the RCA, who had chaired the Design Sub-Group's selection meeting.
Dr Colin Podmore, 8 November 1999

11. In her role as Liturgy and Reference Editor in Church House Publishing, Rachel Boulding became the principal contact between Omnific and the publisher.
12. The Bishop of Guildford (the Rt Revd John Gladwin) was Chairman of the Liturgical Publishing Group and the Bishop Salisbury (the Rt Revd David Stancliffe) is the Chairman of the Liturgical Commission.

The extracts from the Liturgical House Style Guide shown in document 7 are of significance.

DOCUMENT 7

Liturgical House Style Guide. 5th version September 1999

Amen

Amens should always be placed at the end of text on the same line, separated by two character spaces.

Biblical references

· In Bible references, full points should be used to separate chapter and verse numbers, commas should be used to separate verses in the same chapter, and semi-colons should be used to separate out different chapters. The numbers should be closed up, with no space between them, except after a semi-colon.[13]

    John 1.4-6,8-10; 3.1-18

· Hyphens should be used to separate verse numbers within a chapter. En rules should be used where references run across different chapters:

    Mark 10.15-20

    Mark 10–11

    Mark 10.19–11.3

Bold

Bold should always be used for congregational text. Otherwise use bold only when it is essential to differentiate sections of liturgy within a service.

Line breaks

Lines should be determined by sense.

Turnovers are better than lines going into the gutter.

Line spaces

Use half-line spaces between verses in canticles, etc. and between 'or' and 'and' separating sections within the same liturgical texts. Also, half line spaces should be used between rubrics and the liturgical text attached to them. Liturgy can be disrupted by too many full line spaces.

Rubrics

In your manuscript these should be shown in italic. In the published versions rubrics will normally appear in a second colour or sans serif font.

    In general, avoid using a colon at the end of rubrics where possible. If the rubric is a complete sentence, use a full point.

    If the rubric is an incomplete sentence, introducing liturgical text omit all punctuation.

    There is usually a half-line space after the rubric in this case.

13. The rule which specifies 'no space after the comma' is a little unsatisfactory here, causing the number groups to break up.

Section numbers

These tend to make the page look like a table of instructions and so rather messy. They can also be off-putting to those who are not liturgical experts. In deleting them, the font size can be increased, so increasing legibility. The matter is being discussed in Synod and a decision has yet to be made.

A schedule (figure 9) was produced by Church House Publishing and work began on the production of page proofs. Document 8 presents an extract from notes returned with the second proofs (figure 10) of the main volume.

DOCUMENT 8

Edited extract from Rachel Boulding's notes for Omnific, on return of second proofs

---

Common Worship main volume

General

Capitalization: ... Another term to look out for is 'Te Deum Laudamus' – we had asked for 'Laudamus' to be all lower case, but we understand that with the Gill Sans lower case 'l' it would be less clear for the reader, so please search for all occurrences of 'laudamus' and capitalize.

Prelims

Main title page – please use CHP logo and badge, as in Holy Communion booklet. This can be revisited later and discussed further at the next stage.[14]

Collects and Post Communions

Pagination of this section: at present we have some instances of prayers being split across two pages – this only happens over spreads rather than page turns, but please note that it should not happen at all. These occurrences have been marked. There are two rules which we would like to be applied – one is no split prayers, and the other is please start each new season (e.g. Lent) on a fresh page (which you are doing anyway). Within these two rules, please try to fill the pages as evenly as possible. Obviously an under-filled page may occur at the end of a season. We realise that the result will be uneven, but it can't be helped.

Psalter

The pages in this section need to be more evenly filled. I have attempted to suggest revised page breaks, which could have the added benefit of a saving of about 7 pages ... Please make sure that no verse is split within itself across two pages.

14. The CHP logotype was never used on the title page. Omnific did not want to introduce one using a typeface other than that used for the text of the book. The solution was to spell out 'Church House Publishing' in Gill Sans italic.

Sent to us 18/5/00

	**Mon 15/05/00 Common Worship – Main Volume**

ID	Task Name	Duration	Start	Finish	Predec	Resource Names
1	**Editorial stage**	**128 days**	**Fri 14/01/00**	**Tue 18/07/00**		
2	Text to Omnific for typesetting	1 day	Fri 14/01/00	Fri 14/01/00		Jenny Hyatt
3	Liturgical Commission meeting - discussion of editing and presentation of SE & PE	2 days	Wed 02/02/00	Thu 03/02/00		Liturgical Commission, Rachel Boulding, Colin Podmore
4	Education and Communications Sub-Group meeting	1 day	Thu 23/02/00	Thu 23/02/00		Rachel Boulding, Matthew Tickle, David Hebblethwaite, Colin Podmore
5	Liturgical Publishing Group meeting	1 day	Fri 28/04/00	Fri 28/04/00		LPG, Rachel Boulding, Alan Mitchell, Matthew Tickle, David Hebblethwaite, Colin Podmore, Penny Phillips
6	Education and Communications Sub-Group meeting	1 day	Mon 12/06/00	Mon 12/06/00		Rachel Boulding, Matthew Tickle, David Hebblethwaite, Colin Podmore
7	Liturgical Publishing Group meeting	1 day	Tue 18/07/00	Tue 18/07/00		LPG, Rachel Boulding, Alan Mitchell, Matthew Tickle, David Hebblethwaite, Colin Podmore, Penny Phillips
8	**SE page proof stage**	**124 days**	**Tue 11/01/00**	**Fri 07/07/00**		
9	Typesetting of SE	5 wks	Mon 17/01/00	Fri 18/02/00	2	Omnific
10	First proofs of SE to CHP and proofs to proofreaders and indexers	1 day	Mon 21/02/00	Mon 21/02/00	9	Omnific, Rachel Boulding, Penny Phillips, Sarah Roberts
11	First proofs of SE with proofreaders, LC, Focus Groups, etc.	3 wks	Tue 22/02/00	Mon 13/03/00	10	Proofreaders, Liturgical Commission, Focus Groups, Rachel Boulding, Jenny Hyatt, Design Advisory Panel, Penny Phillips
12	Creation of Indexes (Scriptural passages and General)	9 wks	Tue 11/01/00	Mon 13/03/00	9	Peter Andrews, Sarah Roberts
13	Collation of SE first proofs	1.5 wks	Tue 14/03/00	Thu 23/03/00	11	Penny Phillips, Rachel Boulding
14	Indexes circulated to members of the LC for comment	2 wks	Tue 14/03/00	Mon 27/03/00	12	Liturgical Commission, Rachel Boulding, Colin Podmore, David Hebblethwaite, Sarah Roberts
15	SE first proofs to Omnific	1 day	Fri 24/03/00	Fri 24/03/00		Penny Phillips, Rachel Boulding
16	SE first proofs with Omnific for correction	2 wks	Mon 27/03/00	Fri 07/04/00	13	Omnific *(to COE on Mon 10th)*
17	Comments on index to CHP	1 day	Tue 28/03/00	Tue 28/03/00	14	Liturgical Commission, Rachel Boulding, Colin Podmore, David Hebblethwaite, Sarah Roberts
18	Amendments to Indexes by Indexers	4 wks	Wed 29/03/00	Thu 27/04/00	17	Peter Andrews

1

Figure 9. Standard edition (SE) and President's edition (PE) schedule produced by Church House Publishing (CHP). While the schedule was revised many times the final deadline remained unchanged.

Mon 15/05/00 Common Worship - Main Volume

ID	Task Name	Duration	Start	Finish	Predec	Resource Names
19	SE second proofs to CHP	1 day	Mon 10/04/00	Mon 10/04/00	16	Omnific
20	SE second proofs checked	2 wks	Tue 11/04/00	Wed 26/04/00	19	Rachel Boulding, Proofreaders, Liturgical Commission, Design Advisory Panel, Jenny Hyatt, Penny Phillips
21	SE second proofs and indexes collated	1 wk	Fri 28/04/00	Mon 08/05/00	20	Rachel Boulding, Penny Phillips
22	SE second proofs with Omnific and Indexes set	2 wks	Thu 11/05/00	Wed 24/05/00	21	Omnific
23	SE third proofs to CHP	1 day	Thu 25/05/00	Thu 25/05/00	22	Omnific
24	SE third proofs checked	1.5 wks	Fri 26/05/00	Wed 07/06/00	23	Rachel Boulding, Proofreaders, Jenny Hyatt, Penny Phillips
25	SE third proofs collated	1 wk	Thu 08/06/00	Wed 14/06/00	24	Penny Phillips, Rachel Boulding
26	SE third proofs to Omnific	1 day	Thu 15/06/00 *[ON FRI 16th]*	Thu 15/06/00	25	Penny Phillips, Rachel Boulding
27	SE third proofs with Omnific	1 wk	Fri 16/06/00	Thu 22/06/00	26	Omnific
28	SE CRC to CHP	1 day	Fri 23/06/00	Fri 23/06/00	27	Omnific
29	SE final checking of CRC *[4th proofs: to omnific]*	1 wk	Mon 26/06/00	Fri 30/06/00	28	Rachel Boulding, Penny Phillips
30	SE final corrections inserted by Omnific and final checking by CHP	1 wk	Mon 03/07/00 *[5 JULY]*	Fri 07/07/00 *[TO COE 11 JULY]* *[BACK 14 JULY]*	29	Omnific *[DONE/DISC FINISHED 19 JULY]*
31	**Musical Appendix**	56 days	Thu 23/03/00	Thu 15/06/00		
32	Typesetting of Eucharistic Prayers	1 wk	Thu 23/03/00	Wed 29/03/00		RSCM
33	First proofs of Eucharistic Prayers to CHP	1 day	Thu 30/03/00	Thu 30/03/00		RSCM
34	Typesetting of Prefaces	2 wks	Thu 30/03/00	Wed 12/04/00		RSCM
35	First proofs of Eucharistic Prayers with proofreaders, etc	1.5 wks	Fri 31/03/00	Tue 11/04/00		Madeleine Ladell, John Harper, composers, Derek Birdsall, Liturgical Commission
36	First proofs of Prefaces to CHP	1 day	Thu 13/04/00	Thu 13/04/00		RSCM

Mon 15/05/00 Common Worship - Main Volume

ID	Task Name	Duration	Start	Finish	Predec	Resource Names
37	First proofs of Eucharistic Prayers collated	1 wk	Wed 12/04/00	Tue 18/04/00		Sarah Roberts, Madeleine Ladell
38	First proofs of Prefaces with proofreaders, etc.	1.5 wks	Fri 14/04/00	Thu 27/04/00		Madeleine Ladell, John Harper, composers, Derek Birdsall, Liturgical Commission
39	First proofs of Eucharistic Prayers to RSCM	1 day	Wed 19/04/00	Wed 19/04/00		Sarah Roberts
40	First proofs of Eucharistic Prayers with RSCM for correction	1 wk	Thu 20/04/00	Fri 28/04/00		RSCM
41	First proofs of Prefaces collated	1 wk	Fri 28/04/00	Mon 08/05/00		Sarah Roberts, Madeleine Ladell
42	Second proofs of Eucharistic Prayers to CHP	1 day	Tue 02/05/00	Tue 02/05/00		RSCM
43	Second proofs of Eucharistic Prayers checked	1.5 wks	Wed 03/05/00	Mon 15/05/00		Proofreaders
44	First proofs of Prefaces to RSCM	1 day	Tue 09/05/00	Tue 09/05/00		Sarah Roberts
45	First proofs of Prefaces with RSCM for correction	1 wk	Wed 10/05/00	Tue 16/05/00		RSCM
46	Second proofs of Prefaces to CHP	1 day	Wed 17/05/00	Wed 17/05/00		RSCM
47	Second proofs of Prefaces checked	1 wk	Thu 18/05/00	Wed 24/05/00		Proofreaders
48	Second proofs of complete musical appendix collated	2 wks	Tue 16/05/00	Wed 30/05/00		Sarah Roberts, Madeleine Ladell
49	Second proofs of complete musical appendix to RSCM for correction	1 day	Wed 31/05/00	Wed 31/05/00		Sarah Roberts, Madeleine Ladell
50	Complete second proofs of musical appendix with RSCM for correction	1 wk	Thu 01/06/00	Wed 07/06/00		RSCM
51	Third proofs of complete musical appendix checked and final corrections inserted	1 wk	Thu 08/06/00	Wed 14/06/00		Sarah Roberts, Madeleine Ladell
52	Musical appendix to Omnific for insertion into PE	1 day	Thu 15/06/00	Thu 15/06/00		Sarah Roberts, Madeleine Ladell *[no – will come with number 64.]*
53	**PE page proof stage**	60 days	Tue 18/04/00	Mon 17/07/00		
54	PE text based on SE second proofs plus prelims to Omnific	1 day	Tue 18/04/00	Tue 18/04/00		Rachel Boulding

Wed 21/06/00 Common Worship - Main Volume *[PRESIDENTS EDITION]*

ID	Task Name	Duration	Start	Finish	Predec	Resource Names
55	Omnific set new material for PE	2.6 wks	Wed 03/05/00	Mon 22/05/00		Omnific
56	PE first proofs to CHP	1 day	Tue 23/05/00	Tue 23/05/00		Omnific
57	100 new pages proofread. XRs, prelims, indexes and copyright information adjusted	1.5 wks	Wed 24/05/00	Mon 05/06/00		Proofreaders; Indexers
58	PE first proofs collated plus compilation of PE from SE second proofs	3 days	Tue 06/06/00	Thu 08/06/00		Rachel Boulding; Penny Phillips
59	PE corrected first proofs returned to Omnific	1 day	Fri 09/06/00	Fri 09/06/00		Rachel Boulding; Penny Phillips *[Mon 5 June]*
60	Omnific insert corrections from PE first proofs and compile PE	1 wk	Mon 12/06/00	Fri 16/06/00		Omnific
61	PE second proofs to CHP	1 day	Mon 19/06/00	Mon 19/06/00		Omnific *[Weds 14 June →]*
62	PE second proofs checked and final corrections from SE third proofs inserted	1 wk	Tue 20/06/00	Mon 26/06/00		Penny Phillips; Rachel Boulding; proofreaders *[(2weeks) Thurs 15 June → Tues 27 June]*
63	PE corrected second proofs returned to Omnific	1 day	Wed 28/06/00	Wed 28/06/00		Rachel Boulding; Penny Phillips
64	PE corrections from second proofs inserted by Omnific and incorporation of musical appendix *[MUSIC? *]*	1.3 wks	Thu 29/06/00	Fri 07/07/00		Omnific
65	PE third proofs to CHP	1 day	Fri 07/07/00	Fri 07/07/00		Omnific
66	PE third proofs checked	5 days	Mon 10/07/00	Fri 14/07/00		Rachel Boulding; Penny Phillips
67	PE third proofs collated	2 days	Mon 17/07/00	Tue 18/07/00		
68	PE corrected third proofs to Omnific	1 day	Tue 18/07/00	Tue 18/07/00		Rachel Boulding; Penny Phillips
69	Insertion of final corrections by Omnific	3 days	Wed 19/07/00	Fri 21/07/00		Omnific
70	PE CRC to CHP	1 day	Mon 24/07/00	Mon 24/07/00		Omnific
71	PE CRC checked	2 days	Mon 24/07/00	Tue 25/07/00		Rachel Boulding; Penny Phillips
72	**Printing stage**	67 days	Mon 10/07/00	Wed 11/10/00		

179

Mon 15/05/00 Common Worship - Main Volume

ID	Task Name	Duration	Start	Finish	Predec	Resource Names
73	Preparation of PE to printer	2 days	Mon 17/07/00	Tue 18/07/00	64	Katharine Allenby
74	SE at printers	12.2 wks	Tue 18/07/00	Wed 11/10/00	72	At printers
75	PE at printers	12 wks	Wed 19/07/00	Wed 11/10/00	73	At printers
76	**Published books**	31 days	Thu 28/09/00	Thu 09/11/00		
77	Education and Communications Sub-Group meeting	1 day	Thu 28/09/00	Thu 28/09/00		Rachel Boulding, Matthew Tickle, David Hebblethwaite, Colin Podmore
78	Liturgical Publishing Group meeting	1 day	Mon 02/10/00	Mon 02/10/00		LPG, Rachel Boulding, Sarah Roberts, Alan Mitchell, Matthew Tickle, David Hebblethwaite, Colin Podmore
79	Books in warehouse for packing and distribution	4 wks	Thu 12/10/00	Wed 08/11/00	74,75	In warehouse
80	Publication date	1 day	Thu 09/11/00	Thu 09/11/00	79	

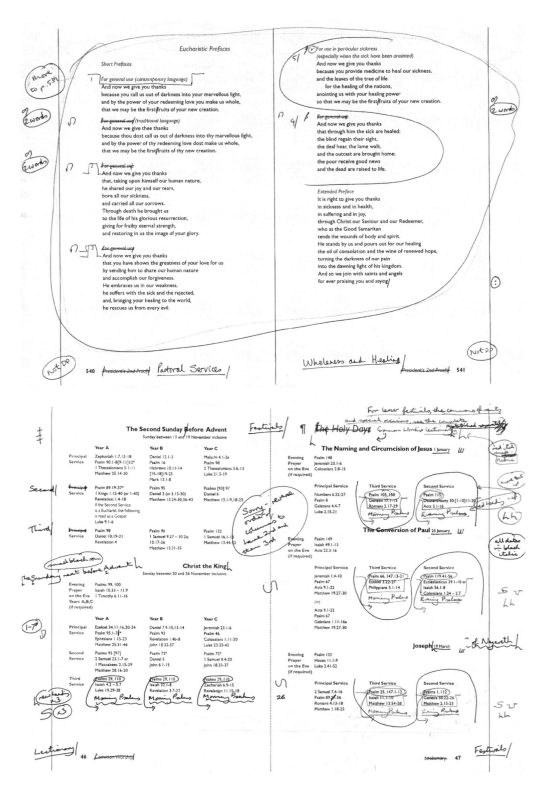

Figure 10. Over 100,000 page proofs
were produced in total, some 12,000
as two-colour laserprinter proofs.
There were six proof-reading stages.
The comments from 14 proof readers
were collated at CHP and corrected by
Omnific. These pages show the still
heavily corrected pages at second and
third proofs.

Throughout the design process, there were regular meetings of the Design Sub-Group. The meeting notes compiled by Dr Colin Podmore, an example of which is shown here, provide an insight into the decision making process.

DOCUMENT 9   21 January 2000

Design Sub-Group Meeting on 20 December 1999

1. Letter from the Revd Colin Lunt
The Sub-Group considered a further letter from the Revd Colin Lunt, in response to the Secretary's reply to his letter in the Church Times, which had questioned the use of Gill Sans as a typeface, but did not consider that the points made were such as to make it an inappropriate choice. [For the text of this letter, see page 56.]

2. Consultation with the RNIB
There were no suggestions for change to the design which the RNIB would wish to press. In particular, the RNIB agreed that red was a preferable colour for rubrics to blue.

The RNIB also concurred with the view that while a serif typeface was more readable for extended passages of text (such as a novel), a sanserif typeface would be clearer and preferable for a book of this kind, where much of the material was in display setting. It was interesting to note that the large-print newspaper Big Print, sponsored by the RNIB, uses a sanserif typeface.

3. Marking of the Holy Communion Services
In deciding to move the Holy Communion services back to a position further into the volume, the Liturgical Publishing Group had asked the Sub-Group to consider whether the pages concerned could be marked in any way – for example by red edging of those pages either all round or merely on one or two edges. The Sub-Group considered the practical and aesthetic aspects of the question and decided that this should not be attempted.

However, it was AGREED that the 'footers' (running feet) and page numbers for the Holy Communion section should be printed in red. This would make them stand out when the pages were turned in search of them.

168 · 394	*Holy Communion*	
168 · 394	*Holy Communion*	
168 . 394	*Holy Communion*	
168	*Holy Communion*	*394*
168	*Holy Communion* . *394*	
168	*Holy Communion*	*394*
394	*Holy Communion*	**168**

4. Separator for dual pagination
It was AGREED that the spaced separator between the two page numbers in the separate booklets and the President's Edition should be a sizeable bold mid-point (similar to a bullet point). This had been recommended as being clearer than a forward slash [see figure 11].

5. Colours for covers

6. Next Meeting
Among the items for consideration will be the physical aspects of the book, such as paper and covers (bearing in mind usage in damp churches and the needs of people with visual impairment and manual dexterity problems).

Dr Colin Podmore, Secretary, 21 January 2000

Figure 11. Trials of dual pagination. The folios for the main volume are in bold throughout. In other editions certain pages carry two sets of folios; the outer 'actual' folios are in roman (regular); the inner folios, in bold, refer to those in the main volume.

DOCUMENT 10   26 January 2000

Extract from Rachel Boulding's letter to Omnific

Psalms: mid verse marker

I have been showing round to people your samples of a mark for the
middle of each psalm verse. There was a surprising degree of consen-
sus in favour of the dot or small bullet point in the top right hand corner of the spread of samples. They felt this was neat and unobtrusive.
Several people felt the ¶ paragraph mark, even if it were smaller, didn't
quite work, being too intrusive and having the meaning of a hard paragraph return.

Could you add another sample, or a few samples in different sizes,
of a diamond, similar to this (as in medieval musical notation). The
Bishop of Salisbury has asked for a third example of a red colon, but
with punctuation at the line ends deleted, except for question marks
[see figure 12].

Figure 12. Psalms mid verse
marker trials.

Psalm 7

1   O Lord my God, in you I take refuge; ¶   you I take refuge; …
     save me from all who pursue me, and deliver me,   ho pursue me, and deliver me,

2   Lest they rend me like a lion and tear me in pieces ¶   like a lion and tear me in pieces …
     while there is no one to help me.   ne to help me.

3   O Lord my God, if I have done these things: ¶   I have done these things: …
     if there is any wickedness in my hands,   edness in my hands,

4   If I have repaid my friend with evil, ¶   friend with evil, …
     or plundered my enemy without a cause,   nemy without a cause,

5   Then let my enemy pursue me and overtake me, ¶   pursue me and overtake me, …
     trample my life to the ground,   the ground,
          and lay my honour in the dust.   our in the dust.

you I take refuge; •   you I take refuge; :   you I take refuge; ··
ho pursue me, and deliver me,   ho pursue me, and deliver me,   ho pursue me, and deliver me,

like a lion and tear me in pieces • like a lion and tear me in pieces : like a lion and tear me in pieces ··
ne to help me.   ne to help me.   ne to help me.

I have done these things: •   I have done these things: :   I have done these things: ··
edness in my hands,   edness in my hands,   edness in my hands,

friend with evil, •   friend with evil, :   friend with evil, ··
nemy without a cause,   nemy without a cause,   nemy without a cause,

pursue me and overtake me, •   pursue me and overtake me, :   pursue me and overtake me, ··
the ground,   the ground,   the ground,
our in the dust.   our in the dust.   our in the dust.

DOCUMENT 11 27 January 2000

Extracts from Publishing Common Worship

Publishing Common Worship (GS Misc 595)
A Further Report by the Liturgical Publishing Group

on behalf of the group
✠ JOHN GUILDFORD, Chairman, 27 January 2000

Informs the Synod of further decisions taken by the group since
November 1999.[15]

B. The Main Volume:

Position of the Holy Communion services

7. There are, however, strong arguments in favour of the Group's
original intention – making the Holy Communion services the second
block, rather than the first, and so placing them further towards the
middle of the book, which was the general intention behind the amendment ... The book will also fall open somewhat more easily at the Holy
Communion services if they are some way into the volume (which is
the reason for the tradition of a more central position).

10. The Design Sub-Group has subsequently decided that the 'footers' (running feet) and page numbers for the Holy Communion services
should be in red, which will make those services stand out when the
pages of the book are turned in search of them, and they will thus be
easier for visitors to find. Furthermore, the book will contain ribbon
markers, which can be used to mark the place to which people should
turn.

Paragraph numbers and common pagination

17. Prof. Frayling reported the strong and unanimous view of the
Design Sub-Group and the designers that paragraph numbers were
both unnecessary and undesirable. The design is notable for its clarity
of print, prominent headings and spacious layout.

18. The Group accepted the view, expressed by a number of Synod
members, that if there are no paragraph numbers, common pagination
between all editions of the book, including separate booklets, is essential. At the same time, it was aware of a widespread view that for a congregation to be asked to 'turn to p. 115', when a service booklet clearly
had a much smaller number of pages and this page was actually the
first in the booklet, was confusing to visitors and tended to reduce the
credibility of the booklet.

19. The Group therefore welcomed the following solution, proposed
by the Design Sub-Group. The separate booklets and the President's
Edition will have dual pagination – a bolder page number beginning
with p. 1, and the page number from the standard edition in lighter type,
separated by a spaced mid-point (comparable to a small bullet point).

15. The Liturgical Publishing Group
had reported its plans for publishing
Common Worship in a report circulated to
the General Synod in October 1999. This
was debated by the General Synod in
November 1999.

Design Sub group
Note of the meeting held on 16 February 2000

Present: Prof. Christopher Frayling, Mrs Alison Baverstock, Canon Jeremy Haselock, Bill Beaver, Rachel Boulding, Colin Podmore Derek Birdsall, John Morgan
Katharine Allenby, Matthew Tickle, David Hebblethwaite[16]

1. Dummies
The Group examined dummies of the books. The following changes/additions to previous plans were agreed:
Standard Edition: red head and tail bands; gold to be brighter if possible; (ribbons to be red and black – confirmed)
Trade Edition: not to have black edging on top;
red&white, blue&white, wine&white head and tail bands respectively; presentation plates, gummed for optional use (to be designed)
Bonded leather: gold edging; head and tail bands as above
four ribbons: gold, red, purple, (dark) green
(the four main liturgical colours)
presentation plates as above
the 'visible line' to be looked at
(if it cannot be removed, the cross must be moved to avoid it)
Calfskin leather: the tan colour to be darker
and more natural – chestnut
head and tail bands red (not striped)
the books to be presented in acetate
the blocking to be looked at
Slip cases: to be plain on the outside, except that the spine would be replicated; simple grey protector slipcase; removable sticker (barcode); the possibility of a purple colour inside to be explored
(printing might be a cheaper option)
Desk edition: red and white head and tail bands
President's edition: red and white tail bands
spine to have the words Common Worship (running down) only, with the badge
Pastoral Services: The words Common Worship: Pastoral Services to appear on the spine, running down. This pattern to be followed for all books of this format other than the main volume desk edition.

2. Separate booklets and holy communion sample edition:[17]
The CHP logo to appear on the back.
matt smooth laminate covers

3. Lectionary section
Two days should be accommodated on each page, divided by a red line (except those days – e.g. Easter – for which there is too much additional material to make this feasible). The names of the lectionaries going down the left hand side of the page to be in red, but the years across the top in black.

Figure 13. A presentation edition of the main volume bound in black calfskin leather with gilt edges.

16. Katherine Allenby (Production Manager) and Matthew Tickle (Sales and Marketing Manager) of Church House Publishing, and David Hebblethwaite (Secretary of the Liturgical Commission), were co-opted as members of the Design panel for this meeting.
17. A sample edition, containing just the services from Holy Communion: Order One, was produced to enable the material and its design to be tried out in the parishes and revised in the light of experience and feedback. A preliminary edition of *Common Worship: Daily Prayer*, published in January 2002, included a questionnaire in which readers are encouraged to record their comments (see figure 14).

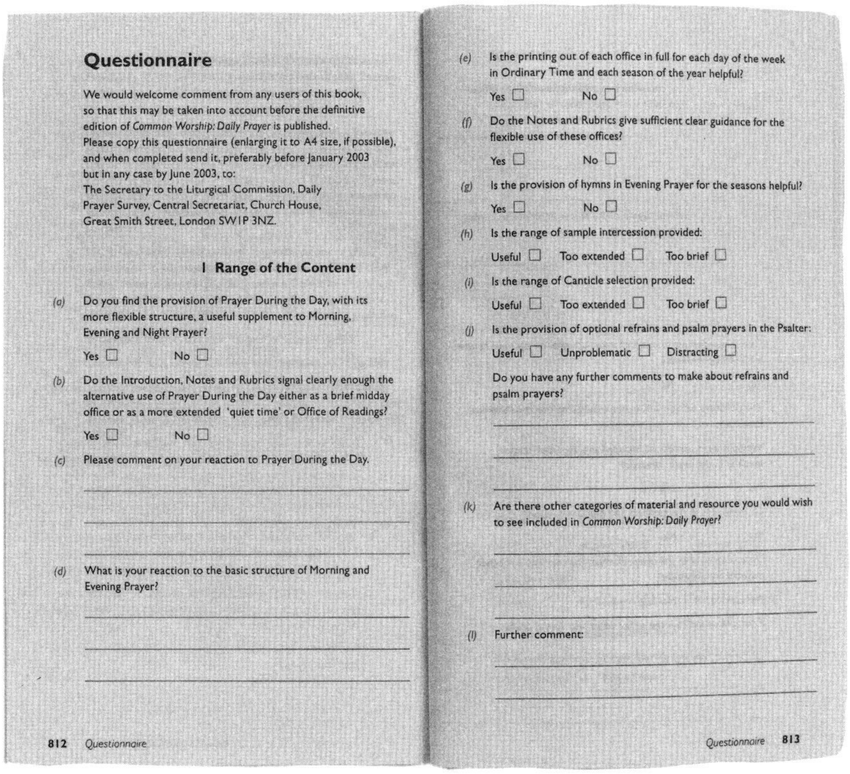

Figure 14. Questionnaire bound into the back of a preliminary edition of *Common Worship: Daily Prayer* (published January 2002) used to 'field-test' the new liturgy.

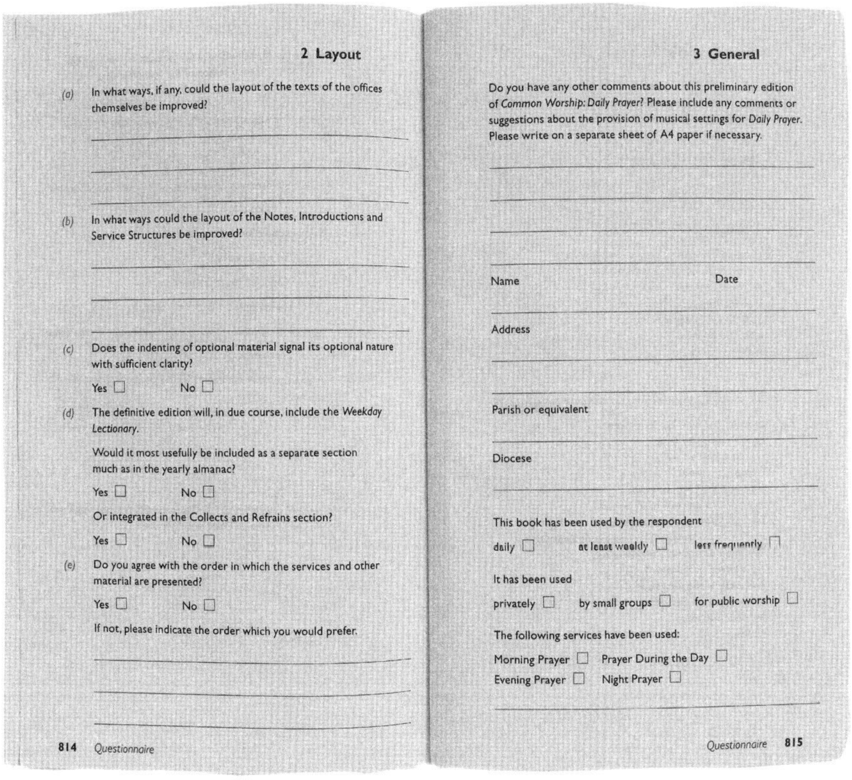

Public responses to the design

One of the most satisfactory aspects of the job was the public debate of content and more unusually the debate over the design outside the design press. There has been a long tradition of parishes designing and producing their own service sheets. While the views expressed in the letters and emails are often questionable, it is remarkable to see typographic debate in the 'non-design' press at all. For that reason alone it is heart-warming.

DOCUMENT 13   25 November 1999

Letter to Church Times

Right typeface for *Common Worship*

From the Revd Colin Lunt

Sir, It was interesting to see a design for the new *Common Worship* material (News, 12 November). The typeface shown in your example looks like Gill Sans, an admirable and "classic" face, but not ideal for large amounts of text. In contrast, the typeface used for the *ASB* has become popular as a text face over the last 50 years because of its excellent legibility.

Perhaps the idea is to make the new material look very different from the old, but legibility should be a top priority. This is to be a liturgical book – every word matters – and it will have to be used thoroughly and repeatedly in situations of poor lighting and distance, not to mention eyesight.

A well-tried text face, such as the Palatino used in the *ASB*, is likely to be more successful than a sans-serif such as Gill Sans. A different face was tried for *Patterns for Worship* and, much as I disliked it (it looks like Cheltenham), I expect it is more legible than Gill Sans. If a different face must be used, how about looking at those in contemporary Bibles? One used in the *REB*, for example, is sharp, distinctive, has a narrowish set, and is very legible. (It looks like Fenice.)

On comparing a copy of the new lectionary (an *NRSV* one from Mowbray) against an *ASB*, I see the new one managed on a larger page size, to use text which is about two-thirds the size of that of the *ASB*. Legibility, legibility, legibility – let's not lose sight of it!

COLIN LUNT

DOCUMENT 14

E-mail from a minister to Matthew Tickle (marketing manager)
following the mailing of the sample booklet

The first people in the parish to be shown the *CW* book were a group of 12–14 year olds at a 'working' picnic lunch. Despite my own prejudices their reaction to its style and appearance was an enthusiastic 'thumbs up', specifically:

Typeface: clearer than *ASB*

Rubrics: red makes a nice change

Layout: more spaced out and nicer to look at

Paper: paper too thin for regular use, it will get scrunched up
and ripped

Paper colour: most liked cream, some preferred white

Cover: looks good, nice and simple, looks 'posh' (I think this translates
into 'has style')

All these comments were spontaneous – I showed them *CW* and the
ASB 'red book' and 'asked what do you think?'

They are desperately keen to help with the design and illustration of
our local (seasonal) booklets.

DOCUMENT 15

From the e-mail discussion list run for Common Worship

COIN (Christians on the internet)

22 April 2000

God must be in the detail, not the devil. This is surely true of typography, as much as theology or anything else.

In too many parishes (mea culpa) poorly produced orders of service
hinder worship and outreach. At the Southwark conference on
Common Worship a couple of weeks ago the point was made that a
great deal of thought (and money) had gone into the appearance of the
new services, and that parishes should use the typography of the new
book as a model of good practice. Many parishes produce their own
service booklets, and it was strongly hinted that they should aspire to
the standards of the new prayer book.

Eric Gill worked (often in an unorthodox way) to glorify God.
Choice of type is not merely an 'arcane' or worldly detail, it should be
an expression of the Divine (I'd argue Gill Sans is just that), as much
as the words used. It can be a help (or hindrance) to us as we move
towards an apprehension of the Divine.

A publisher friend commented that the *Common Worship* sample
booklet could have been designed by Gill himself. I agree, and think
that's a cause for great joy. Why should the devil have all the best
tunes?

I thought my posting would be merely helpful and uncontroversial!
I say churchwardens should keep their noses out of such matters!

A peaceful Easter to all

Stephen Black, Churchwarden, St Andrew, Coulsdon

29 October 2000

Much more colourful once you open the book – black and white,
flashes of red and purple, and a touch of gold – a pretty good combination of colours, I think, and could be said to symbolise the CofE at
its best.

Sheila

2 November 2000

I have read with interest the postings about the use of Gill Sans in the recent communion book. We are told that this is to be the font used in Common worship material. I am a great fan of Gill Sans (and its creators Johnstone and Gill), and it has enjoyed a revival amongst designers in recent years. But I wouldn't use it as a bodyface. By the way, serif faces *are* easier to read. Try putting a ruler over the descenders of a serif and a sans serif face. It is not just a matter of design preference.

Why not keep to Stone Sans and Stone Serif, as used in *CLC* and Initiation Services, which I thought had established the Common Worship look (just as Palatino established the *ASB* look)? They were an excellent choice, and I would be sorry if they have been ditched. Is this another case of the CE being unable to make up its mind?

Typoholically yours

Mark Cuming

On 21 April 2000, Stephen Black wrote:

Gill Sans, again …

Mac-users should try 'Capel-Y-Ffin' before giving the Monotype Corporation their money. According to the designer it is 'designed to resemble Gill Sans' (it *certainly* does), though 'it is not the equal of commercial versions' (true), 'but beats doing without by a long shot' (*definitely*).

You can download it from 'Mac Font Vault' www.erik.co.uk/font/ It's on the sans serif menu and is $5 shareware.

It certainly doesn't have the refinement of Gill Sans (the numbers are not right – the zero is downright too big, and the italic doesn't quite make it). Nonetheless it is far more convincing than some of the alternatives suggested here.

Stephen Black

Why are we getting so excited by fonts – gill sans – and all the other arcane details? – why not use what suits you and your parish – or have I missed something?

Cedric Catton

Music

Music for the Eucharistic Prayers was included at the back of the President's edition. It consisted of two groups of settings: settings using the traditional chant melodies (using a lower case Gill Sans 'g' clef) (see figure 15); and three examples of new settings especially prepared for *Common Worship* (using a more conventional clef). Further special settings were published by the Royal School of Church Music.

Figure 15. (right) The 'g' clef as devised by John Harper at the Royal School of Church Music.

Figure 16. (below) A page spread from the service booklet designed by Omnific for the inauguration of the Seventh General Synod in November 2000, when the new *Common Worship* Holy Communion service was used for the first time. Illustrates a full integration of music setting and an appropriate centred text alignment for the processions.

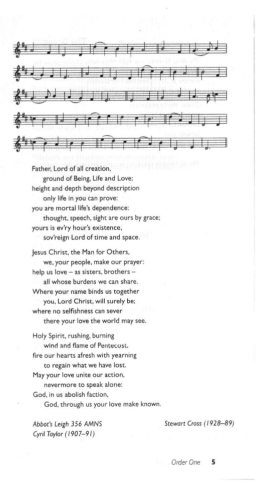

Electronic products

Common Worship material was published in the *Visual Liturgy* 3.0, the latest version of the service and worship planning package. Its layout reflects that of the printed text while it allows the reader to produce customised services, choose alternative texts, create overhead transparencies, link automatically to Bible texts and more.

In addition to *Visual Liturgy*, the *Common Worship Text Disks* were designed for those who cannot run *Visual Liturgy*. The text disks contain the full texts of all material from the main volume and Pastoral Services in RTF text files.

All of the liturgical texts were also made available free of charge on the Web in three different formats – RTF, PDF and HTML. The Bishop of Guildford explained one of the reasons for this to the Synod as follows, 'We are of the opinion that, rather than leaving these matters to others, it is our task to take the lead in making our work available. That fits with one of our key principles, which is to do all we can to ensure that, whenever and wherever the Church's liturgies are made available, they are in a form which is consonant with the purpose of those liturgies and in a form which is both lawful and accurate.'[18]

Print production[19]

The printing contract was placed with Cambridge University Press, which has a distinguished history of printing bibles and prayer books dating back to 1588. Cambridge sub-contracted the long run (300,000) standard edition to Splichal, a bible printer based at Turnhout in Belgium which had both the expertise and the web presses most suited to producing two-colour, high quality work on Bible-weight papers. No British printer was able to produce all the *Common Worship* editions to the specifications within the time available. The fine bindings and larger formats were all produced at Cambridge.

The Standard and Desk editions were printed on 55 gsm Primapages Ivory, a new paper made on the shores of Lac Leman, France.

The President's edition was printed on 100gsm Dutchman Ivory, specially made in Holland to match the shade and surface of the Primapages paper. The individual booklets are printed on 80gsm and 100gsm Dutchman Ivory respectively. The purple endpapers throughout are a special making of GFSmith's Colorplan.

All editions are thread-sewn, with head and tail bands and bound in one of three materials: Miradur, a plastic-covered imitation leather; Cabra, bonded leather; and calfskin. The slipcases for the presentation editions are covered in Kephera, a material which changes colour slightly where blind-blocked at 200°C.

18. *General Synod Report of Proceedings*, vol. 30, no. 2 (November 1999), p.323.

19. Printing and binding specification:
Standard Edition
300,000 copies printed web-offset in 2 colours by Splichal, Belgium, on 55 gsm Primapages Ivory: 200k bound in Miradur imitation leather at Splichal. 50k bound in Cabra-bonded leather and/or in calfskin (slip-cased) at Cambridge University Press from book-blocks supplied by Splichal. 50k held as sewn book-blocks for later binding in varying styles. Two ribbons.
Pastoral Services
10,000 copies printed sheet-fed in 2 colours on a Roland Ultra by Cambridge University Press, on 55 gsm Primapages Ivory, and bound in Miradur imitation leather. Four ribbons
President's Edition
7000 copies printed sheet-fed in 2 colours on a 5 unit Speedmaster by Cambridge University Press on 100gsm Dutchman Ivory. 4k bound in Miradur imitation leather, slipcased; 2k Calfskin art-gilt on 3 edges (red under gold), slip cased; 1k held as book blocks for future binding. Six ribbons.
Desk Edition
7,000 copies printed sheet-fed in 2 colours on a Roland Ultra by Cambridge University Press, on 55 gsm Primapages Ivory. 6k bound in Miradur imitation leather, slip cased; 1k Calfskin, gilded, slipcased. Four ribbons.
The series of booklets containing individual *Common Worship* services, produced concurrently with the main books, were printed and bound by ArklePrint, Northampton.
In addition, a series of booklets containing specific services from the main volume were required in two formats. These were rationalised as 202 × 125 and/or 250 × 155 mm; Holy Communion Order One (64pp)
Holy Communion Order One in Traditional language (48pp)
Holy communion Order Two (32pp); Holy Communion Order Two in Contemporary language (40pp); Morning and Evening Prayer from *The Book of Common Prayer* (48pp); Morning and Evening Prayer on Sunday (72pp); Night Prayer (Compline) (16pp); Night Prayer (Compline) in Traditional language (16pp); Marriage (48pp); Ministry to the Sick (88pp); Funeral (80pp); Lectionary Advent 2000 to the eve of Advent 2001 (72pp); Four Services were required in card format. This size was rationalised as 250 x 125 mm (the same width as the standard edition but taller to economise on pages/folds)
Holy Communion at Home or in Hospital Order One (4pp)
Holy Communion at Home or in Hospital Order Two (4pp)
Thanksgiving for the Gift of a Child (4pp); The Baptism of Children (6pp).

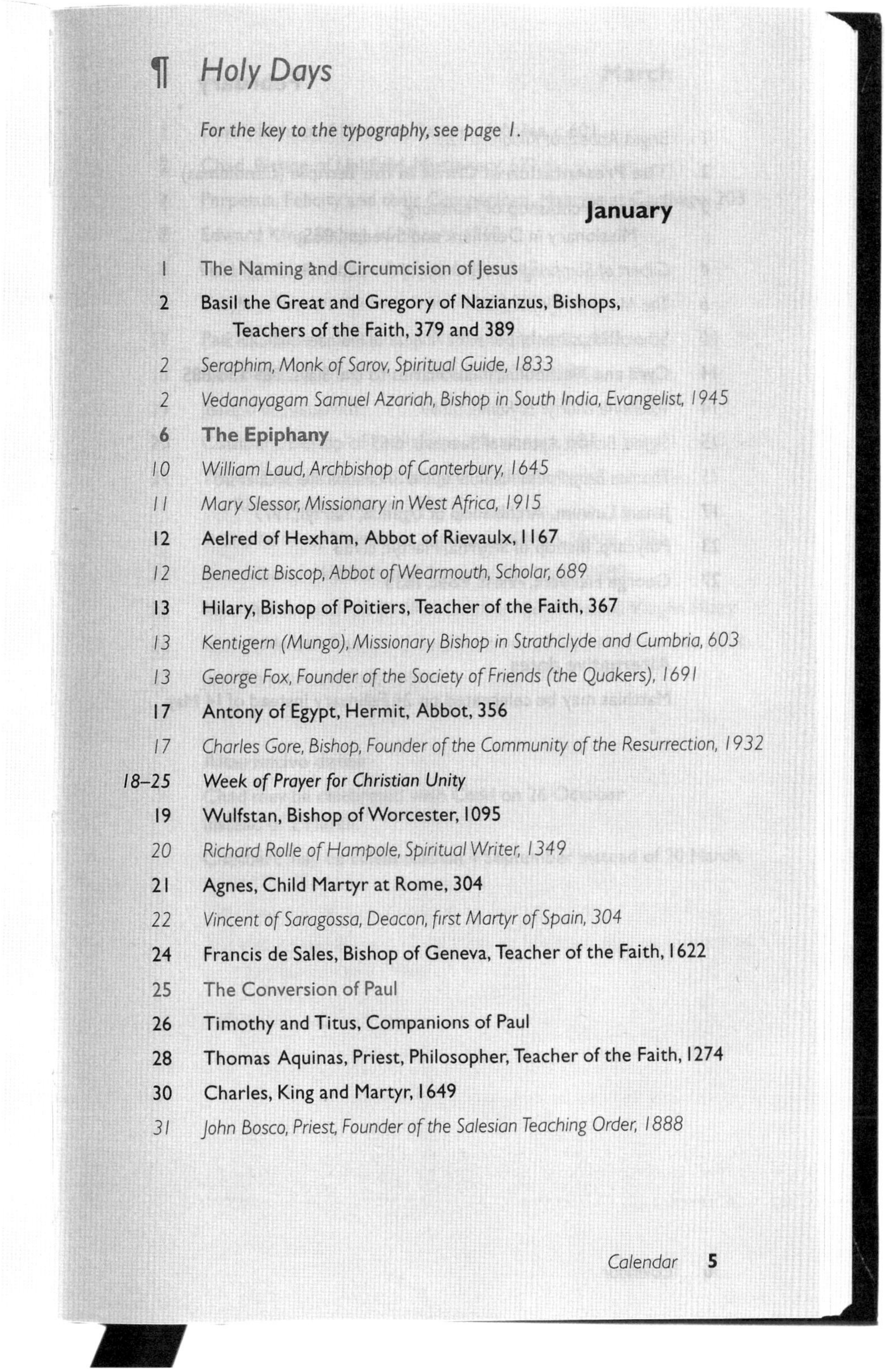

¶ *Holy Days*

For the key to the typography, see page 1.

January

1	The Naming and Circumcision of Jesus
2	**Basil the Great and Gregory of Nazianzus, Bishops, Teachers of the Faith, 379 and 389**
2	*Seraphim, Monk of Sarov, Spiritual Guide, 1833*
2	*Vedanayagam Samuel Azariah, Bishop in South India, Evangelist, 1945*
6	**The Epiphany**
10	*William Laud, Archbishop of Canterbury, 1645*
11	*Mary Slessor, Missionary in West Africa, 1915*
12	**Aelred of Hexham, Abbot of Rievaulx, 1167**
12	*Benedict Biscop, Abbot of Wearmouth, Scholar, 689*
13	**Hilary, Bishop of Poitiers, Teacher of the Faith, 367**
13	*Kentigern (Mungo), Missionary Bishop in Strathclyde and Cumbria, 603*
13	*George Fox, Founder of the Society of Friends (the Quakers), 1691*
17	**Antony of Egypt, Hermit, Abbot, 356**
17	*Charles Gore, Bishop, Founder of the Community of the Resurrection, 1932*
18–25	*Week of Prayer for Christian Unity*
19	**Wulfstan, Bishop of Worcester, 1095**
20	*Richard Rolle of Hampole, Spiritual Writer, 1349*
21	**Agnes, Child Martyr at Rome, 304**
22	*Vincent of Saragossa, Deacon, first Martyr of Spain, 304*
24	**Francis de Sales, Bishop of Geneva, Teacher of the Faith, 1622**
25	The Conversion of Paul
26	Timothy and Titus, Companions of Paul
28	**Thomas Aquinas, Priest, Philosopher, Teacher of the Faith, 1274**
30	**Charles, King and Martyr, 1649**
31	*John Bosco, Priest, Founder of the Salesian Teaching Order, 1888*

Calendar **5**

Figure 17. A page from the Calendar in the standard edition illustrates the necessity in choosing a typeface with an extensive family. Almost all the variants of Gill Sans are used here. Principal Feasts and other Principal Holy Days are in printed in bold (red); festivals are printed in roman/regular (red); other Sundays and Lesser Festivals are printed in roman/regular (black). Commemorations are printed in light italic.

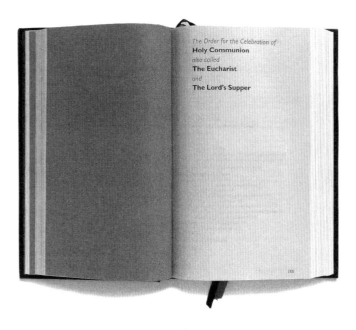

Figure 18. Several variations are played on the basic structure of the central column with margins on each side, including two- and also three-column setting.

Various refinements were made during the design process. The large italic and secondary bold sub-headings were reduced from 16pt to 15pt, and 12pt to 11pt respectively. The bold (11pt) sub-headings were ranged right on the (backed-up) left-hand margin. The 9pt italic rubrics were enlarged to 9.1pt to bring them nearer in appearing size to 9pt roman.

The Church was ready to drop the word 'All'. Omnific suggested it should keep its place. It was essential that each spread should be self-contained, and that the reader did not need to be familiar with the rules to be able to speak when necessary and without fear or embarrassment. Besides, when repeated fearlessly the red italic 'All' becomes a decorative device.

Psalm 58

1 Do you indeed speak justly, you mighty? ♦
  Do you rule the peoples with equity?

2 With unjust heart you act throughout the land; ♦
  your hands mete out violence.

3 The wicked are estranged, even from the womb; ♦
  those who speak falsehood go astray from their birth.

4 They are as venomous as a serpent; ♦
  they are like the deaf adder which stops its ears,

5 Which does not heed the voice of the charmers, ♦
  and is deaf to the skilful weaver of spells.

6 Break, O God, their teeth in their mouths; ♦
  smash the fangs of these lions, O Lord.

7 Let them vanish like water that runs away; ♦
  let them wither like trodden grass.

8 Let them be as the slimy track of the snail, ♦
  like the untimely birth that never sees the sun.

9 Before ever their pots feel the heat of the thorns, ♦
  green or blazing, let them be swept away.

10 The righteous will be glad when they see God's vengeance; ♦
   they will bathe their feet in the blood of the wicked.

11 So that people will say,
       'Truly, there is a harvest for the righteous; ♦
   truly, there is a God who judges in the earth.'

Psalm 59

1 Rescue me from my enemies, O my God; ♦
  set me high above those that rise up against me.

2 Save me from the evildoers ♦
  and from murderous foes deliver me.

3 For see how they lie in wait for my soul ♦
  and the mighty stir up trouble against me.

4 Not for any fault or sin of mine, O Lord; ♦
  for no offence, they run and prepare themselves for war.

Acknowledgements
Thanks to Derek Birdsall at Omnific and Colin Podmore at Church House for reading an earlier draft. Special thanks to Paul Stiff for his encouragement and kind editorial suggestions.

Common Worship: A COLOPHON

Omnific (design & typesetting)
Derek Birdsall
Elsa Birdsall
Shirley Birdsall (née Thompson)
John Morgan

Church House Publishing
Alan Mitchell *Publishing Manager*
Katharine Allenby *Production Manager*
Rachel Boulding *Liturgy and
  Reference Editor*
Hamish Bruce *Publications Officer*
Christina Forde *In-house Designer*
Rebecca Froley *Electronic Editor*
David Green *Marketing Executive*
Ray Green *Production Controller*
Sheridan James *Marketing Executive*
John Kanes *Copyright and Contracts Officer*
Tracey Messenger *Editor*
Penny Phillips *Liturgy Editor*
Sarah Roberts *Editorial Manager*
Matthew Tickle *Sales and
  Marketing Manager*
Aderyn Watson *Publishing Assistant*

Music
John Harper *Royal School of Church Music*
Alistair Warwick *Royal School of
  Church Music*

Website
Simon Sarmiento

Printers
Cambridge University Press, Cambridge
Splichal, Turnhout, Belgium

Bibliography

This article is based in large part on notes from Derek Birdsall, Colin Podmore, Katherine Allenby and exhibition captions produced by Omnific for the exhibition *Common Worship: Design and production*, at the St Bride Printing Library, London, in November 2000. The job archives for the *ASB* and *Common Worship* are held at the St Bride Printing Library. In the following list, the place of publication is London unless otherwise indicated.

Bradshaw, P. (ed.), *Companion to Common Worship, volume 1*. 2001: Society for the Promotion of Christian Knowledge (SPCK)

Common Worship, Services and Prayers for the Church of England. 2000: Church House Publishing

Common Worship, Planning for change: suggestions and ideas. 2000: Church House Publishing

Crutchley, Brooke, *To be a printer*. 1980: The Bodley Head, London

Earey, Mark (ed.), *Producing your own orders of service*. 2001: Church House Publishing

General Synod Report of Proceedings, vol. 30, no. 2 (pp. 321–336). 1999: Church House Publishing

Kinross, Robin, '*Common Worship*: chapter & verse', *Baseline*, no.33, 2001

Morison, Stanley, *English prayer books: an introduction to the literature of Christian public worship*. 1943: Cambridge, Cambridge University Press

New Liturgy for the Church of England is coming soon ..., Church House Publishing, 2000

Publishing Common Worship: *Report by the Liturgical Publishing Group* (GS 1355), 1999: General Synod

Publishing Common Worship: *a further report by the Liturgical Publishing Group* (GS Misc. 595), 2000: General Synod

Rogers, Bruce, *An account of the making of the Oxford lectern Bible*. 1941: Philadelphia, Lanston Monotype Machine Company

Eric Kindel

Recollecting stencil letters

This essay is a recollection of stencil letters and associated artefacts of the past four centuries. It begins with a brief definition of stencil letters and a review of their presently known historical applications, then focuses on three inter-related factors that contribute to the forms of stencil letters. These factors are 'methods of manufacture', 'use' and 'design'. The discussion is guided by documents and references that address stencil letters and the stencilling of texts and other graphic matter, by the analysis of extant artefacts, and by insights gained through reconstructions.

author's address
Department of Typography &
  Graphic Communication
The University of Reading
PO box 239
Reading RG6 6AU
England

e.t.kindel@reading.ac.uk

Nearly everyone is familiar with stencil letters. They are in fact so common that, beyond the few enthusiasts who find them of interest, their familiarity discourages our attention until we re-discover their usefulness in circumstances where nothing else serves so well. For anyone who wants to know more about stencil letters than might be hit upon simply by using them, information does come to hand, though not much. When stencil letters are discussed, they typically play only a minor part in a larger story: as a style of printing type or a letter for signs, as an industrial vernacular adopted by avant garde artists, architects and designers, as *matériel* of warfare, and so on. If encyclopedias offer entries on stencilling, emphasis is commonly placed on the application of colour to playing cards or the decoration of interiors and only rarely on marking out letters and words. When manuals for stencilling and screen printing assemble a history of the technique by way of introduction, their accounts of lettering are erratic in scope and accuracy. But occasionally, stencil letters figure prominently. This is true in articles about liturgical books made with stencils. And once in a while a stencil letterer or signwriter will publish a record of their own efforts. The work they reproduce is often ingenious while the practices they describe are (as we will see) proof that many aspects of stencilling are historically persistent. More commonly though, their interests bypass historical matters, or address stencilling mostly as a means of illustration.[1]

If such texts are gathered up, a view of stencil letters emerges, but one that is fractured and in many places wholly obscured. So it is not difficult to assert the need for a fuller history, one that draws together a body of examples and practices that are in themselves worthy of investigation, and whose study will also elucidate the intersection of stencil letters and stencilling with typography, printing, letter design and multifarious trade-crafts whose stories are better known. That said, the present essay will not attempt a fuller history; but as a first step, what follows is a recollection of stencil letters from a variety of periods, made in different ways for many purposes. The intention is to map out

1. Hutchings (1965: 23–6) is the most comprehensive review of stencil letters manufactured as printing types; this inventory is based on an earlier article (1958). Discussion of stencil letters in the context of twentieth-century avant garde art can be found in many works, though Marcus (1972) is a good starting point, as is Miller (1993). Volumes listing artefacts of the American Civil War for collectors and re-enactors, such as Phillips (1974: 138–40) or Sylivia and O'Donnell (1978: 282–3), illustrate a variety of stencils and related tools used during that conflict. Tomlinson (1854), a typical trades encyclopedia, lists stencilling but only to direct the reader to information under playing cards; more recently Rickards (2000: 311–2) includes a useful entry on stencilling in the context of (printed) ephemera. Twentieth-century writers on stencilled liturgical books include Schreiber (1927: 174–5), O'Meara (1933), Gottron (1938), Rodrigues (1973) and Rosenfeld (1973); they variously refer to earlier commentators, among them Heinecken (1771: 270–1), Breitkopf (1801: 32–3), Fischer von Waldheim (1800–4: 139–60), Jansen (1808: 34–41) and Lacroix (1852: 56–7). Saudé (1925), Hunter (1946: 143–57) and Abbe (1980) are all records of individual practice though Saudé documents *pochoir*, stencilling that is often associated with (book) illustration and decoration in the late nineteenth and first half of the twentieth century.

stencil letters by way of their form and the factors that contribute to it. The discussion will begin with a general description of the stencil letter, but thereafter concentrate on examples found specifically in the work of stencilling. An examination of form means that local practices of stencil-making and use will be addressed only where they demonstrate particular points; a representation of the diversity of practice is not envisioned. But by emphasizing issues of form, the recollection should provide a basis for subsequent, detailed discussions elsewhere on specific episodes of practice within this fascinating sphere of letters.[2]

What is a stencil letter?[3]

The technical principle of stencilling is so simple it hardly merits explanation, though for the sake of describing stencil letters, a short review is needed. To create a stencil, a design is pierced or cut out from a sheet (or 'plate') of metal, card, paper, plastic or some other flat material. Thereafter, the design is transferred to a surface by passing ink or pigment through the stencil's openings.[4] The process, of course, requires that no ground be isolated within the figure of the design as this enclosed ground would fall away when the stencil is made. Stencil letters, then, are those that may be used for stencilling. In keeping with the figure-ground arrangement just described, stencil letters have no ground that is entirely enclosed within the figure of the letter; or put slightly differently, the ground within and around the letter is always entirely contiguous. It is this attribute that all stencil letters share, with several important exceptions.[5] But letters that can be used for stencilling are not always so employed: they can be applied by other means; or cut out and left at that. So to advance a description of stencil letters, their formal attributes should at first be summarized without reference to stencilling.

A series of two-dimensional letters (figure 1, a–h) illustrate how the contiguity of ground just described is achieved.[6] In some instances, letters are constructed from simple elements that are discrete and unjoined, i.e. individual (often modular) elements arranged to indicate a letter, though each element remains isolated from the others (a). Next, letters are described as having 'breaks' in their construction, but in a manner that is less an arrangement or repetition of individual elements and more sections of an overall form kept separate (b, c). Distinguished from these are letters whose construction incorporates breaks to produce a contiguity of ground, though the original form of

2. Throughout this essay, I usually refer only to 'stencil letters', for convenience. But the stencil letters so called often include many more characters as found, for example, in a (single weight) fount of printing type. Because practices of stencil-making and supply vary widely, it has seemed best to adopt this somewhat general description except where the character set needs to be stated more precisely.

3. This question was suggested by 'What is a typeface?' (Kinross, 1986).

4. The design may also be transferred by other means, such as light.

5. Exceptions include letters that are pur-

posely designed to disguise their stencil attributes. Letters of this kind are split into two or more parts where the ground of each part is entirely contiguous. When they are rejoined to make the complete letter (through consecutive printings, for instance) this contiguity is lost as ground is enclosed within the figure of the letter. Two-colour letters may be designed in a similar manner, if not necessarily with the same intention; the type Bifur ('double' variant; A. M. Cassandre, 1929) demonstrates this. Other exceptions that should be mentioned are the letters used in stencils made of transparent film, as found in photo-reprographic screen printing or in the

manufacture of dry transfer letters using master patterns cut from multi-layered masking film (Brignall and others, 1996). Here the figure of the letter is supported by, or fully part of a substrate that need only allow the transmission of light; contiguity of ground is thus technically irrelevant.

6. In the descriptions that follow, the demonstration of contiguity will refer primarily to those letters whose ground is conventionally discontiguous: A/a, B/b, D/d, e, g, O/o, and so on; it is, however, common for the formal attributes that provide contiguity to be applied to all letters even if some do not strictly require this.

a. Johann Merkenthaler, from an advertising circular, *c.* 1900
b. Bery (*c.* 1781)
c. Hunter (1946)

d. Richford (*c.* 1920)
e. Johann Merkenthaler, from an advertising circular, *c.* 1900
f. Bauer (*c.* 1760)

g. Marsh (*c.* 1947)
h. Helvetica modified

Figure 1. Contiguities of ground. a–g reproduced at actual size from source given; note that dates refer only to the sources named and not necessarily to a date of design, which may be earlier.

7. The approach to description and some of the terminology used here are derived from Dixon who, in creating a framework for describing typographic letters, lists the visual, formal attributes of types (in two dimensions) and identifies their sources and influences. An attribute Dixon gives for some types, and one that proves helpful in the context of stencil letters, is 'broken/interrupted'. It describes 'clear breaks in character construction', but may alternatively refer to shape or decoration where a 'cut-out' or 'subtraction' alters or embellishes an existing form. ('Broken/interrupted' also describes the emphatic points of transition found in the construction of broken-script letters, i.e. 'blackletter' or 'gothic'; this sense is not intended here.) See Catherine Dixon, 'A description framework for typeforms; an applied study', PhD thesis, London: Central Saint Martins College of Art & Design, 2001.

the letter was probably unbroken (d–g). Here, modifications range from those sympathetic to the underlying letter to those where no apparent effort has been made to integrate the break into the overall design; instead, it bluntly joins interior and exterior ground. More extreme modifications involve simply removing or filling in the interior ground (h).[7]

The illustrations shown in figure 1 are only selected locations in a continuum of stencil form; individual examples must be examined – often closely – before an accurate description of their contiguity of ground is possible. Indeed some letters incorporate several tendencies and so require a more elaborate description. But once the fundamental attribute of contiguity is confirmed, the description of a stencil letter should be supplemented by components that identify its other formal attributes. For example, if a stencil letter has been through a process of modification in order to achieve its contiguity of ground, many of the descriptive components will identify the attributes of the original underlying letter. Similarly, for stencil letters principally derived from decorative elements, the elements should be named and listed. In all the examples given so far, no specific reference to the activity of stencilling or to the physical artefact of a stencil is necessary.

Having described the stencil letter in its two-dimensional state, a third dimension can be introduced; it locates the stencil letter's physical form. When a two-dimensional stencil letter without a specific context is cut from some material, the letter becomes space defined by the edge of the material; or rather it pleasantly alternates between space with a material boundary, and material whose edge creates the letter. Perhaps it is more productive (and less bewildering) to consider space and matter as two inseparable parts of a whole. When describing a stencil letter in three dimensions, it is helpful to introduce a new term, the 'bridge', to replace the breaks of the two-dimensional letter. It suggests a three-dimensional construction that joins separate areas. But

Figure 2. Friendly society pole head ('BS'=Benefit Society[?]), brass, England (West Country; specific provenance unknown), *c.* first half 19th century, Museum of English Rural Life, The University of Reading.

Figure 3. Stencil, punched brass, North America, late 19th/early 20th century. Actual size.

Figure 4. Figure 3, as stencilled.

bridges are more than the source of contiguity: they give strength and structural integrity to the pierced or cut-out material.[8]

The precise context of the stencil letter is now the remaining component of description to be added. As mentioned, stencil letters are found in contexts that are unrelated to stencilling (figure 2); but for those that are stencilling-specific, they occur in several places. Most common is the stencil (figure 3): it carries the letter and anticipates the activity of stencilling. But the stencil letter is elsewhere too, if more obscurely; for instance, at the end of steel punches used to cut stencils. The punch is an intermediary: it holds or stores the letter for cutting; another intermediary is a pattern that guides a pantograph. In any case, once the stencil is made it gives rise to the *stencilled* letter, that is to say, one made by stencilling (figure 4). In this state, the letter has returned (more or less) to two dimensions and though it is described accordingly, it often gains additional attributes from its manner of application and from the surface it has been applied to.

The stencil letter is thus a transient entity, shifting from two dimensions to three, from space to solid matter, from future possibility to past act. Adding to its mutability is the very descriptor 'stencil letter' whose technical reference is sometimes irrelevant or, if not, may refer to multiple states.[9] But the name is the one most commonly understood and a qualified, orderly application of it can usefully delineate the stencil letter's many visual and material forms.

Sources, context and factors of form

Despite the variety of contexts in which stencil letters are located, the discussions that follow will focus solely on stencil letters found in the work of stencilling. This is to illustrate the often close association that exists between the form of the stencil letter and how it is made and used for stencilling. To understand this association, I have collected evidence from a range of sources. Most important are the artefacts of stencilling itself: stencils and the tools and materials related to their manufacture and use; and works made with stencils: books, specimens, commercial documents, signs and much else. Significant too are printed ephemera: catalogues, broadsheets, flyers, packaging, trade cards and other items that describe and illustrate how stencils were made, sold and used. Further evidence is gathered from documents, both published and unpublished, that describe working practices. Some are first-hand accounts, compiled by stencillers, stencil-makers or by observers; others are second-hand, where the authors have taken a specific interest in stencilling but have not necessarily made observations for themselves. Collateral sources supply contextual information on relevant technical and aesthetic developments.[10]

8. There are a number of terms used in the past to describe that which ensures contiguity in the stencil. The earliest so far found is in Des Billettes (*c.* 1700). He refers to this element as a *tenon*, or 'attachment'; the verb is *tenir*, or 'to hold'. Jansen (1808) relies on *le réserve*, a term denoting those elements which, in any process of making a print or executing a design, are left blank or untouched by ink, paint, acid, and so on. In

English, in 1811, the connecting ground is a 'tie', as in 'common ingenuity might overcome the difficulties of O and other letters by ties' (quoted in Rhodes & Streeter 1999: 129; the context is duplicating texts using stencils; see also note 32 below). Tie may be the most common term, used more recently in Hunter (1946), Hutchings (1965) and Abbe (1980). 'Bonding' is more idiosyncratic, adopted by Mackenzie (1950), while O'Meara (1933)

prefers 'bridge', as do I.

9. Dorothy Abbe remarks: 'Actually, one *stencils* a *stencil* and the product is a *stencil*' (Abbe, 1980: 3n.); emphasis in the original.

10. Although I have gathered sources and artefacts from as broad an expanse of time and location as possible, they are far from comprehensive and should be considered only indicative, not representative. Additions are anticipated and welcomed.

11. Early dates are from Des Billettes (*c.* 1700) and Fischer von Waldheim (1800–4): the former (discussed below, note 14) suggests *c.* 1620–60; the latter quotes a reference (147n.) of 1674 naming a deceased Trappist monk who in life cut stencil letters (*La Trappe Fr. Benedictus des Champs piissime obiit, qui in vitâ suâ literas laminis incidit*). Fischer von Waldheim offers a lengthy 'pre-history' for stencil letters, i.e. before the development of the stencilled liturgical book. He asserts that stencils were sometimes used for marking out royal monograms and signatures (Justinian, Theodoric, Charlemagne) and for (decorated) initials in early printed books. Reaching further back to antiquity, he cites a passage from Quintillian (*Institutio oratoria,* 1, 1, 27) on the teaching of writing to children; this, he concludes, was done with stencils. Doubt is cast over most of these assertions by Rosenfeld (1973) who instead postulates connections between decoration, the manufacture of playing cards, and stencil lettering that may have contributed to the latter's exploitation for making liturgical books.

12. A distinction should be made between the largely manual and low-volume or 'one-off' stencilling referred to here (and throughout this essay) and stencil duplicating, a semi-mechanical species of screen printing developed later in the nineteenth century primarily for copying documents. See Proudfoot (1972) and Rhodes & Streeter (1999).

13. e.g. Econosign (UK) or Stencillor (US). A vernacular tradition of signwriting with stencil letters also persists in parts of France, commonly using letters adapted from the modern face roman.

To provide some historical orientation for the development of stencil letters, the narrative these sources suggest should be briefly sketched out. An early programmatic application of stencil letters in Europe first occurs in the seventeenth century, when they were used to mark out texts in liturgical books.[11] In work of this kind, texts were often combined with stencilled initials and other decorative matter, guided by the conventions of printing and typography, and to a lesser degree the illuminated manuscript. Such books and the brass or copper stencils used for them were usually made in workshops and scriptoria in northern France (principally Paris), Germany (the Mainz region especially), Flanders, and Italy (Rome) but possibly elsewhere too and in other settings. They are often magnificent in format, graphic expression and craftsmanship, made singly or in small multiples for private individuals or for group worship and chanting in monastic or church services. The use of stencilling for large-size liturgical books and for smaller format devotional literature and secular works was probably most common in the latter half of the eighteenth century and the early years of the nineteenth, and it was during this period that the technique attracted the attention of printing historians. In addition to books, stencils were used to apply scriptural texts to walls, probably as part of ecclesiastical or domestic decorations; and no doubt they were employed in other related contexts where letters were needed.

The earliest known commercial maker of letter stencils was working in Paris in the 1780s, though it is probable that others were already in operation well before then. In the late eighteenth century, merchants in France and England, and artists and engineers in German-speaking areas (Breitkopf, 1801: 33) were using founts of single character stencils, or stencils carrying words and decorations; and by the early nineteenth century, billheads, receipts, labels and other ephemera were 'printed' in small multiples with them.[12] At this time, stencils were made by specialists or by engravers producing lettering work of several kinds, but as the nineteenth century progressed they were more commonly made by companies offering a variety of marking devices. Stencil use continued to grow in the second half of the nineteenth century in areas such as agriculture, bulk packaging, shipping and the military, and in domestic settings, particularly for marking names, monograms and decorations onto linen. Patent specifications for many and various stencil-related inventions were filed at this time, especially in the United States, some of which automated stencil manufacture. It may be that in Europe and North America stencilling letters was never more popular.

Over the last one hundred years, the use of stencil letters has continued in shipping, heavy industry, construction and the military but lessened elsewhere as other methods of marking have replaced stencilling. Similarly, the stencilling of letters and graphic matter in small businesses has also declined, despite occasionally regaining a degree of popular application, for instance in do-it-yourself signwriting kits of the 1920s and later.[13] For the purposes of domestic decoration, stencilling remains widely used though lettering does not often figure in it. Rather, the stencil letter is more likely to be found in non-stencilling contexts – avant garde art, type design or architectural signing – where

14. Many of the observations to follow on early stencil letter cutting are taken from this important source. Around or just before 1700, Gilles Filleau des Billettes compiled a lengthy draft text describing various aspects of printing (Des Billettes, *c.* 1700). It was a contribution to the 'Commission Bignon', formed under the authority of the French Royal Academy of Sciences to survey the *arts et métiers* of France beginning with printing and its related trades. (For a summary of the Commission's work see Jammes (1965) and Mosley (1995) and (1997).) Des Billettes' text contains a section of some 10,000 words headed 'Printing of church books, scriptural texts or maxims etc.' relating to the production of liturgical texts using stencils. He describes the construction of special furniture, tools and stencil letters needed for such work, and a procedure for using them systematically. An engraving by Louis Simonneau, dated 1701, illustrates the description. While it appears that this section of Des Billettes' text is more nearly a proposal than a record of contemporary stencilling practice, it is probable that some of the details he supplies were based on observations in the field. Notably, at the start of the section, Des Billettes surmises that the use of stencils for marking out texts had evolved from several trade practices (not mentioned) 40 to 80 years earlier and that its 'invention' could not therefore be attributed to a single source. I am indebted to James Mosley for bringing this unpublished text to my attention (see Mosley, 1995, III: *388–90n. and *394n.) and for consulting on its study, as it falls within his own expertise and work on documents produced by the Commission Bignon. The text has also formed the basis of a separate research project I have conducted with consultation from Andrew Gillmore, James Mosley and Fred Smeijers. The project reconstructed and tested the stencilling apparatus and procedures described by Des Billettes and some of its findings are drawn on here.

15. *On prend des plaques ou des lames de cuivre c'est a dire du laton bien minces, et autant qu'elles peuvent l'estre en gardant quelque consistance pour la durée et qui puisse soustenir le travail qu'on y doit faire, et celuy de leur usage.* (English translation in text by James Mosley.) Commenting on the terminology found in the French, Mosley writes (in correspondence with the author): '*Cuivre* at this period may mean "copper" but in the context of tools and made objects it almost invariably means "brass". The term *laton* means "thin brass", a little thicker than "foil", and there is an [analogous] English term "latten". *Plaques ou lames* both mean "plates"; a *lame* would be thinner than a *plaque*, and the end of the sentence makes it clear that the very thin brass known as *laton* is what is meant.' See also

innovations in its form are made, if free of some or all of the exigencies that are the subject of the present essay. But isolated examples of stencilling give evidence of continued experiment and renewal, as in the clandestine inventions of stencilled graffiti and rogue advertising.

From the narrative of practice just sketched, and from the sources and artefacts that describe specific episodes, it is possible to identify a group of factors that contribute most to the forms of stencil letters produced over the past several centuries. While the factors might well apply to any prefabricated letter, in the context of stencil letters they are certainly apt. First, design is signally important. Design, however, does not refer only to the stencil letter's final visible form, but to underlying models, guides, antecedents and conventions, and to strategies of designing that draw on them. Next are the materials from which the stencil is made and the tools and working methods employed in its manufacture. These are essential to the realization of the stencil letter, aiding the intentions of design or presenting obstacles that encourage certain forms and not others. And once the stencil letter is designed and made as a stencil, the vagaries of skill and purpose in its handling and application further add to the letter's final form by rendering it accurately or altering it wilfully or ineptly.

Design, manufacture and use, then, provide divisions for discussion (though not in this order). But while each factor on its own emphasizes a particular dimension of stencil letters, it is essential to see the three factors as knit together, often closely. In the sections that follow this is understood implicitly, and acknowledged explicitly where possible.

Manufacture

Cutting

The simplest way to make a stencil is to cut it by hand with scissors, knives, chisels or other cutting tools. Historically, cutting may be the most commonly-practised method as it can be conducted quite informally, often with few special skills. It was certainly used early in the period under review.

According to Des Billettes (*c.* 1700),[14] cut stencil letters were made of brass: 'one takes pieces of very thin brass of the kind called "latten", as thin as they can be while keeping the strength that will make them last and stand up to the work that must be done with them.'[15] The use of brass depended on its ready supply as pre-made sheets in a variety of gauges or as thicker pieces to be hammered flat; Des Billettes suggests that brass in these formats was conveniently available. To make stencils 'last and stand up', the qualities of brass were quite suitable. Its strength facilitated the work of cutting and refining the letters while its resilience meant that stencils could easily withstand the repeated brushing, wiping, washing and drying they would endure. Such advan-

Mosley (1995, III: *358–9) where several of these and other related terms are discussed in the context of typefounding. A note inserted by Des Billettes into this sentence as it appears in the original MS gives the optimum thickness of the *laton* as a twelfth part of a *ligne*, i.e. a *ligne seconde* (*c.* 0.188mm) the basic unit of measurement in the first scheme of

proportional type bodies devised in 1694 by Des Billettes' colleague Jean (Sébastien) Truchet for the Commission Bignon (Mosley, 1997: 11). While in the context of stencil-making this specification may seem little more than a borrowed convenience, it is in fact a quite suitable thickness for sustaining the work of cutting and filing.

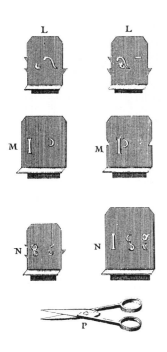

Figure 5. Stencils, from an engraving by Louis Simonneau (detail), 1701, depicting a suite of stencilling equipment as described in Des Billettes (*c.* 1700). From the album 'Les Arts et Métiers de l'Académie des Sciences', St Bride Printing Library, 5825. Note that only the lower right stencil approximates the format described by Des Billettes; cf. figures 6 and 31.

16. The use of brass may be set against paper, card or canvas coated with varnish or oil paint, materials already well established in the work of stencilling colour onto prints and playing cards. If also employed for stencilling letters early on, these materials might be found in contexts where resilience or longevity were not especially important or where a good deal of customized design was needed for a specific application. Equally, paper, card or canvas would perform well, and no doubt economically, where large-size letters were required but would not facilitate fine detail in small letters. Rosenfeld (1973: 77) speculates that copper stencils were used for the mass production of playing cards and that some influence would have been felt by early stencil letter cutters through this channel. Some early nineteenth-century commentaries on stencilling (e.g. Jansen, Sievers) name copper as a common material for stencils and it is indeed found in examples of the

tages surely justified the expense of time, effort and materials that brass stencils required; and the investment could be recouped over a long working life.[16]

On cutting the letters, Des Billettes offers a brief description. The operation began by inscribing four lines across the uncut plate, corresponding to the height of the capital, the x-height, the baseline and the descender depth. Guided by these proportions, the outline of the letter was also inscribed on the plate.[17] Next, the plate was punctured within the outline using pointed scissors which were subsequently deployed to snip away the letter, working outward from the puncture. Any roughnesses or areas the scissors were unable to reach were removed and refined with files of various shapes and sizes, or with a knife. Des Billettes notes that the files were those of the clockmaker and so implies his expectation that the letters be refined and well-finished (figure 5). But Des Billettes did not think letters cut and finished with scissors, knives and files could be well-formed or easily used below a certain size. He counsels the would-be stencil-cutter: 'sizes will be few in number as one cannot make the characters [very] small, and it would be very difficult or at least quite useless to make any as small as *gros parangon* [*c.*22 point Anglo-American], because even if they could be well executed, there would be even more difficulty in marking them out properly.' Instead he recommends *gros canon* (*c.* 44 point) as the smallest size that should be attempted.

In stipulating a stencil letter's smallest effective size, Des Billettes asserts a relationship between the form of the letter, the tools and techniques employed to cut it in brass, and its eventual use. The relationship is one of mutual restraint among the factors just listed. But rather than simply accept Des Billettes' assertion unreservedly, it might be more instructive to test his way of working, and so articulate the attributes of the cut stencil letter more fully.[18] To begin with, he confidently recommends scissors for cutting the brass plate. For large-size letters, scissors alone might be effective if their points are sharp and the brass they are cutting is thin. Attributes of form that can result from their use include awkward or irregular curves. But for small-size letters scissors are essentially ineffective as they bend the plate when snipping the letters out. Knives, too, are relatively inconvenient for cutting brass of the thickness Des Billettes specifies. An alternative is a set of chisels shaped to cut the various curves and straight parts of letters. Surprisingly few are required and may be struck though brass with ease. Attributes of form produced by curved chisels can include poorly-joined points of transition from curves to straight sections, and the recurrence of the same curve in several parts of the letter or among different letters. Straight chisels often produce a series of small nicks in the brass along the outline of a letter and can result in faceted curves.

nineteenth century and later. However, pure copper is less appropriate for stencils than brass, an alloy of copper and zinc: although copper is softer and easier to cut, it is less resistant to deformations caused by forceful or clumsy handling, brush pressure during use, or even heat generated from rubbing. Deformations such as warping or bending can significantly impair a stencil's performance.

17. Des Billettes says little more about the design of the letter or how, exactly, it was inscribed on the brass plate prior to cutting. The implication is that the outline was freely made; he describes the work variously with the verbs *tracer* (to draw or trace) and *dessiner* (to draw or design).

18. Statements that follow in this paragraph are based on trials and observations made by Fred Smeijers.

Figure 6. Stencil, cut with short straight chisels and finished with files, brass; and (at right) letter as stencilled. Actual size. Cut by Fred Smeijers, 2002, based on Des Billettes (*c.* 1700); see also figure 31.

Both kinds of chisels give rise to sharp, pointed features, serifs especially (figure 6; see also figure 31).[19] The other tool Des Billettes recommends, the file, is useful regardless of how the stencil is cut and would, in its different profiles, contribute much to the letter's well-regulated form. In fact the file may smooth away those traces of scissors and chisels just mentioned. And his prediction of the smallest possible letter size also appears well-founded. This, however, is determined less by use (the 'difficulty in marking them out properly' is contentious) but rather by the nature of the tools: files and scissors may not fit within the outline of a letter while chisels are difficult to align and control at small sizes. So a degree of caution should accompany Des Billettes' account of the tools and procedures he thought most suitable for cutting stencils, though the attributes he suggests and those just postulated can help in identifying stencil letters made in this way.

Commentators on stencilling in the century and more after Des Billettes offer little help in resolving these matters: their accounts are sketchy or ambiguous. Nearly all identify sheets or plates of brass or copper as the most common materials for the stencil; none mention paper, card or canvas. Little else is said about how the stencils were made and it can only be assumed that cutting was the principal method used. Nor do their choice of words make conclusions any easier. For instance, Fischer von Waldheim (1800–4), who wrote from first-hand knowledge of stencilled liturgical books made in the Mainz region, describes the stencils as cut (from *schneiden*) without naming the tools or procedures involved. He does mention a monk (see note 11 above) working in the seventeenth century who 'cut letters in plates' (*literas laminis incidit*).[20] Breitkopf (1801: 33) was told that stencils made in Paris were 'pierced by hand' while Jansen (1808), writing in French, only offers a generic description of cutting (from *découper*). Sievers (1825: 357) is more forthcoming in his description of work in the Papal (Sistine) Chapel in Rome. There, stencils for liturgical books were made from thin copper sheets and he lists the tools used: 'chisels, shears, rulers, set squares, compasses and the like, [such] that one would believe oneself in a locksmith's and copper engraver's work-shop.' His list implies cutting and his failure to mention any unusual or

19. It may be significant, in the context of Des Billettes' account, that in French 'chisels' and 'scissors' share the same word: *ciseaux* (rendered *cizeaux* in the MS); Des Billettes, however, is clearly referring to scissors.
20. Fischer von Waldheim (1800–4: 147n.); cf. Jansen (1808: 39n.).

Figure 7. Stencil, knife-cut [?] brass,
Germany, *c.* late 19th/early 20th century. Actual size.

Figure 8 (right). Stencil, chisel-cut
(wholly or in part) brass, North
America or Britain, *c.* 19th century.
Actual size.

Figure 9. Stencil (detail), chisel-cut
zinc, North America, *c.* 19th century.

21. Late 19th- and early 20th-century
catalogues indicate that letters three
inches or greater in height were cut by
hand, for example Quint (*c.* 1887–95), The
Wharton Novelty Co. (*c.* late 19th c.) and
Hoep (*c.* 1939); the tool used is not named.
Spencer (*c.* 1890) describes the letters of
made-to-order stencils as 'chiseled [to]
any special shape or to fit any given space
wider or narrower than the ordinary letter'. Incidentally, Hunter (1946: 156)
advises that when the signwriter is asked
to supply lettering as metal stencils, the
letters should first be drawn on paper and
pasted onto a metal (copper, lead or zinc)
plate. The stencil is then made by pressing
a knife through the plate in a series of short
cuts.

more technically sophisticated method encourages the supposition.
But these descriptions are discursive and should be treated with caution. Each commentator's admiration for books made with stencils
came at the expense of recording specific technical details and
procedures. They were, however, agreed on the fluency of what they
observed: Sievers describes the letters he saw as 'cut to the greatest
perfection'; Fischer von Waldheim and Jansen emphasize the stencil's
delicacy of form, as if surprised by it; and Breitkopf remarks on the
evenness of the letters he examined.

After these equivocal written sources, further attributes of cutting
are more readily ascertained by examining a series of stencils whose
letters were probably made in this way. Although later in date (nineteenth or twentieth century), they are likely to have attributes similar
to earlier work. The first example is a monogram (figure 7) apparently
cut with a knife. Because of its delicate and complex forms, it is
uncommon to find a monogram stencil made in this way. But its small
size and narrow openings suggest the possibilities and limitations of
cutting at this scale. A second example (figure 8) is a stencil cut wholly
or in part with straight and curved chisels. This is especially evident in
the serifs whose similarly shaped curves make awkward transitions into
the strokes, a fault characteristic of chisel work. One further example
illustrates a large-size letter cut from zinc using a single short chisel.
The chisel's residual marks are here left in the metal (figure 9).[21]

In addition to identifying attributes of the stencil letter cut with
scissors, knives, chisels and similarly simple tools, it is also worthwhile

Figure 10. Stencilled letters,
W.A. Dwiggins, original stencils are
knife-cut celluloid, United States,
c. 1930s–50s.

22. Abbe (1980); Dwiggins was highly
proficient at such work. He employed
stencils in the late 1920s to construct orna-
mental motifs, mostly for books, and for
making letters, as he was also an accomplished letterer, calligrapher and type
designer. Cut from celluloid with a short-
bladed knife, his stencil letters have a fluid-
ity that would be difficult to achieve in
metal. See also Brignall and others (1996).
In a related matter, in the late 1920s or
early 1930s, Dwiggins corresponded with
Eva Judd O'Meara, librarian of the music
library at Yale University, on the subject of
stencilled liturgical books, about which
O'Meara was then preparing an article
(O'Meara, 1933). She solicited Dwiggins'
views on how quickly and easily a choirbook (Boddeart, 1755) owned by Yale
might be marked out and Dwiggins'
opinion is given in her article (faster than
writing, he thought).

23. Hind (1963: 105)

24. Set of brass stencils in walnut box
(Museum Collections); related items
include: specimen sheet of Bery (Franklin
Miscellaneous Collection B:F85.93);
receipted bills (Franklin-Bache Papers
BF85.ba, including December 29, 1781
(PH58 1p) and January 12, 1782 (PH62 1p));
and 'Account of family expenses begun
March 15, 1779' (Franklin Papers
F85f6.22); see also Lingelbach (1948:
92–5).

to summarize the general circumstances that might encourage this way
of working. As it is relatively inefficient and without any significant
technical challenges, cutting would, with few exceptions, be common
where rapid and specialized mass-manufacture was unimportant, and
especially appropriate for work that required stencils for 'one-off'
applications or commissions. And if, as might commonly be the case,
the stencils were not to be sold, their making might be as rough or precise, as conventional or unusual as necessary. Furthermore, cutting
would recommend itself to work done at large sizes and, by implication, with inexpensive or disposable materials. Echoing several elements of this summary is the work of William Addison Dwiggins, who
cut stencil letters in a wide range of sizes (figure 10). Many of his letters and alphabets were designed and made for his own satisfaction and
personal use, or for graphic design commissions. They, together with
his tools, materials and methods of work, demonstrate the informality
and invention of stencil work based on cutting.[22]

Etching

While stencil letters cut with simple tools may, through ingenuity and
manual fluency, achieve a considerable measure of sophistication, some
cannot be made in this way and for them another, more technically
advanced method is required: etching. With etching, stencil letters of
almost any form are possible. They may resemble those made by cutting or some other method of manufacture, but in general etching generates letters whose forms are smaller, finer or more elaborate. To
observe and describe etched stencil letters is, of course, important in
elucidating the likely procedures brought to the work. But the compilation of attributes shared by etched letters is also important in simply
identifying them as such – an often difficult task if the stencils themselves cannot be examined. When a stencil letter can be confidently
identified as etched, it allows the technical expertise attained in an
associated stencil-making context to be established, something of
considerable value to the description of early stencilling practices.

Etching stencil letters from metal probably dates to the first half of
the eighteenth century, though possibly earlier. Before its use in stencil-making, etching is found from at least the fifteenth century in gold-
smithing and in other trades involved in metal-engraving.[23] While in
some instances artisans employed etching only to mark the surface of
metal, as in the decoration of armour, elsewhere it pierced the metal to
create 'cut' work. It is not difficult to extrapolate the application of
etching to stencil-making: a thin sheet of copper or brass would offer
little resistance to a penetrating mordant and so a stencil letter might
be generated with ease and accuracy. That etching was the basis of
stencil-making towards the end of eighteenth century is established by
a quite extraordinary survival from this time. It is a set of stencils –
more than 400 – made by Bery whose Paris workshop was located on
the pont Notre Dame. The set was purchased by Benjamin Franklin
in 1781 while he resided at Passy as a United States diplomat to the
French court and is accompanied by a specimen sheet that advertises
Bery's inventory of stencil letter designs and sizes (figure 11). The
entire collection remains among Frankin's effects gathered by the
American Philosophical Society in Philadelphia.[24]

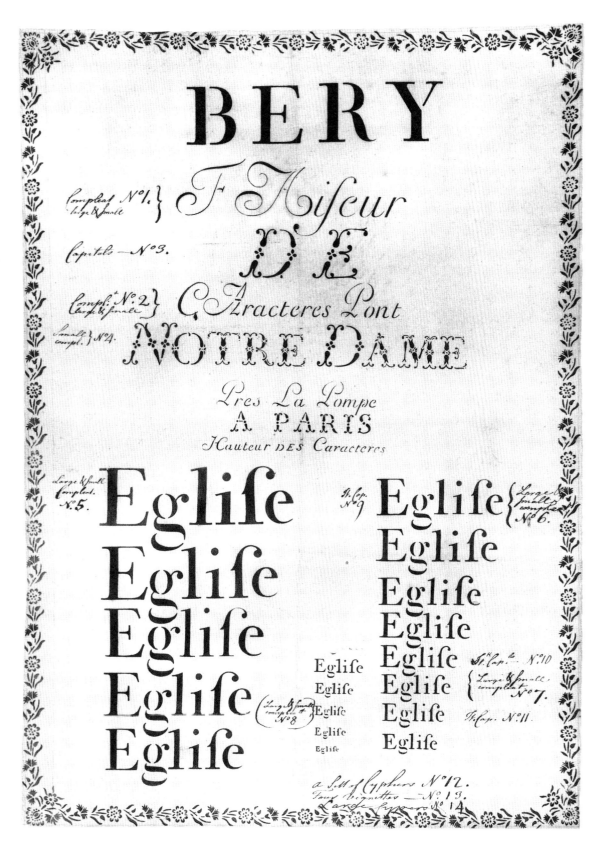

Figure 11. Stencilled specimen sheet of Bery, Paris, *c.* 1781, reduced to 50 per cent linear. Library of the American Philosophical Society, Philadelphia.

Figure 12. Stencils of Bery, etched
brass, Paris, *c.* 1781, American
Philosophical Society, Philadelphia.
Actual size.
a. No. 1: script (*bâtarde coulée*)
b. No. 4: decorated
c. No. 6: large roman, with spacing dot
d. No. 8: small roman, with spacing
dot and maker's marks
(Numbers given refer to specimen
sheet annotations in figure 11)

When reviewing the work of Bery, what is striking is as much the
expertly designed letters as their highly proficient realization as stencils. The precision with which the complex forms perforate the lumi-
nous orange-yellow brass plate demonstrates a craft in a considerable
state of advance (figure 12, a-d). In fact the stencils are so well made
that there are few obvious indications of just what procedures were
employed. The brass shows no evidence of cutting with scissors, knives
or chisels, either freely or to an inscribed outline. Nor is any filing
noticeable to refine and smooth the edges of the letters. The absence of
such features in particular, and the extraordinary fineness of the stencils in general, point to etching as the only method likely to produce
such results.

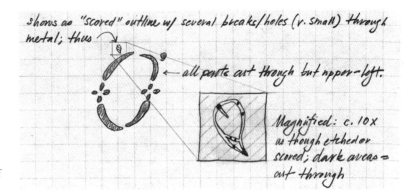

shows as "scored" outline w/ several breaks/holes (v. small) through metal; thus

← all parts cut through but upper-left.

Magnified: c. 10x as though etched or scored; dark areas = cut through

Figure 13. Sketch of O, from no. 3 of Bery specimen sheet.

But exactly how the letters were etched is less clear. Fortunately, one error remains that betrays at least part of the procedure (and further confirms the use of etching). It is found in the stencil of a large-size decorated O. A curved teardrop element at the upper-left of the letter is not removed from the brass plate as intended. Instead, its outline is etched but incompletely: sometimes to a shallow depth, elsewhere penetrating through the plate. Other partly etched lines are also visible crossing within the element (figure 13). This residual error suggests that the letter's outline was inscribed using a template – possibly another stencil. If a previously made stencil did function as a template, then the work might procede as follows: an etching ground would be laid onto the plate to be etched; the template, laid over it, would guide an etching needle scribing through the ground on the plate beneath. A mordant, set onto the plate thus inscribed, would etch along the exposed brass and eventually cut through it. The brass within the outline would fall away (or be pushed out) leaving the space of the letter. Such a procedure, or one like it, explains the inscribed and etched element embellishing the O, its interior still *in situ*, and may be applicable to the other stencils Bery produced. It is, however, only a fragment of some larger process of work whose other features are less obvious if not wholly uncertain.[25]

As a means of generating stencils singly and repeatedly, templates are convenient and efficient. And if it is difficult to ascertain the complete process of work Bery employed, it is easy to assert the advantages of etching in general. In the first instance, it makes almost any form possible at any size. Bery was clearly aware of this and so made numerous roman and italic letters in a great range of sizes, scripts of considerable swash and flourish, and decorated capitals whose delicately cut tendrils and blossoms hardy seem plausible in the context of stencil-making. But it is not just fineness in form-making that etching allows; the process also has few adverse effects on the brass plate itself. Unlike a cutting tool, the action of the mordant is free of forces that distort or bend the plate. In addition, etching may be performed on a group of plates simultaneously and thereby encourages a kind of mass production – not truly so, but certainly by comparison to cutting. Perhaps it made commercially viable Bery's many letter sizes, or his decorated designs aimed at eighteenth-century tastes. In the latter instance, a relationship might even exist between a demand for letters and other decorative material of this kind and the exploitation of etching to supply them as stencils.[26]

25. Remarks made here are based on discussions with Fred Smeijers. Other possible features of template work should be briefly noted. One is the production of an 'original' template. This might be done by freely inscribing a letter into an etching ground laid on a blank plate, then etching the plate; or by employing an inscribing guide made of reinforced paper (a 'pre-template'), its letter drawn by hand or adapted from an engraved letter or a printed type, and cut out with a knife. A second feature of template work involves the correct location of a template over the plate to be inscribed. Residual marks on the Bery stencils may offer some insight: baselines are inscribed across almost all of the stencils and possibly helped locate template positions. But intriguingly, some stencils in the Bery set carrying the smallest sizes of letter (nos. 7 and 8 as marked on the specimen sheet) are also inscribed with x-height, capital/ascender-height and descender-depth lines as required. Their presence undermines the use of templates as their only apparent function would be as guides for letters scribed freely on the plate.

26. The Bery set also includes several large, decorative border stencils (*c.* 70 × 190 mm) carrying fleurons or other modular motifs; each design includes an integrated corner element.

Figure 14. Stencilled letters, decorated, by U. Boddaert, from 'Graduale Romanum de Tempore & Sanctus' (detail), Flanders: Abbey of Loo, 1755, reduced to *c.* 50 per cent linear. Gilmore Music Library, Yale University, New Haven.

Figure 15. Stencilled decoration with handwriting, from 'Chronologie des rois de France depuis Pharamond', 1751, reduced to *c.* 35 per cent linear, Wing MS 60. Courtesy of the John M. Wing Foundation, The Newberry Library, Chicago.

Given the sophistication of the Bery stencils, it is likely that etching was already practised before the 1780s. Though no stencils contemporary to or earlier than his are known that might prove this, indications are provided by stencilled books. For instance, in Boddeart's 'Graduale' of 1755 decorated letters are used extensively (figure 14). In his dedication, he describes the letters as made from brass sheets carved or engraved with outlines *(formulis insculptis laminis aereis)*. While the description is ambiguous, the detail of Boddaert's letters, in the light of Bery's work, suggests etching. So does another book, a royal genealogy made in Paris in 1751 (figure 15). On each of its pages, decorated borders and *fleurs-de-lis* frame written matter. The borders are of similar detail and complexity to those Bery made as stencils. And

Figure 16. Stencilled choirbook, page
from 'Antiphonarium Carthusiense',
made by Pater Thomas Bauer,
Mainzer Karthause, *c.* 1760, reduced
to *c.* 32 per cent linear.
Stadtbibliothek-Mainz, Hs. II 137.

27. The stencil work of Pater Thomas
Bauer, a monk at the Carthusian
monastery in Mainz, was regarded by
Fischer von Waldheim as the most accomplished he had seen. Bauer is thought to
have been a student of Johann Claudius
Renard, also a highly accomplished stenciller who moved to Mainz from Lüttich in
the 1730s. Renard subsequently conducted
workshops and supervised stencil work at
a number of monasteries in the region.
Bauer's stencilled liturgical books survive
in Mainz at the Museum-Gutenberg and
the Stadtbibliothek. See Fisher von
Waldheim (1800–4), O'Meara (1933),
Gottron (1938), Rodrigues (1973),
Rosenfeld (1973).

in other stencilled books from the middle of the eighteenth century, the
forms of the letters and the decorative material that accompanies them
are such that is difficult to imagine how the stencils used to mark them
out were made other than by etching (figure 16).[27]

It is probable, then, that etched stencils were increasingly common
in the second half of the eighteenth century in Paris and further afield.
Beyond the contexts of secular and ecclesiastical book production,
however, their application is not easy to gauge. Little stencilled
ephemera from the eighteenth century is known; what is known con-
sists of pharmaceutical labels, bookplates and visiting cards. All were
generated from stencils whose letters or decoration appear to have
been etched. But in addition to fine and detailed forms, another
attribute of such artefacts may also signal the use of etching: the
arrangement of several graphic elements in a single stencil, rather than
just one character. Decorative borders were perhaps the first instance
of large and graphically elaborate stencils. However a *carte de visite*
designed by Bery, with the legend 'Mr Franklin' surrounded by a sinuous border, demonstrates more clearly how a variety of letters and decorative elements were brought together to form a composite design for
a specific function, to be marked out repeatedly as needed. In the first
half of the nineteenth century, billheads, stationery, library and product labels, bookplates and visiting cards were all produced by stencils

Figure 17. Stencilled heraldic device,
bookplate of Samuel Wilton Rix,
England, *c.* early to mid 19th century.
Actual size.

Figure 18. Stencilled monogram,
bookplate of William Kirby, England,
c. late 18th century. Actual size.

whose complexity points to a method of manufacture capable of finesse
and efficiency in equal measure (figures 17, 18). It is among these
instances of stencil-making that etching would prove itself suitable,
even essential.

By the second half of the nineteenth century, stencil-making
increased significantly and etched stencils from this period survive in
large numbers. They are typically thin and fine, made of copper or
brass (sometimes zinc) and often carry – like their eighteenth-century
forebears – letters, monograms and decorative material of considerable
delicacy and detail (figure 19).[28] Their manufacture, whether by specialist stencil-makers, engravers or larger companies, also appears to
incorporate a procedure wherein the letter is etched along its outline
(figure 20). The transfer of the letter onto the blank plate was probably
done manually at first, though eventually a photomechanical process
may have performed this task. Some stencils were clearly batch-
produced from a single large plate later cut into pieces, as confirmed

28. These stencils are less than 0.10 mm
thick; they were typically used in gentle circumstances: to stencil a design onto linen as a
guide for embroidery. Despite the light handling they probably received, the plates were
prone to cockling when used on a soft cloth
surface and many that survive are bent
inward with broken bridges.

Typography papers 5 2003/65–101

Figure 19. Stencil, etched brass or copper, Johann Merkenthaler, Nuremberg, *c.* late 19th/early 20th century. Actual size.

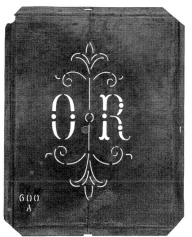

Figure 21. Stencil, etched brass or copper, Johann Merkenthaler, Nuremberg, *c.* late 19th/early 20th century. Actual size.

Figure 20. Stencil (detail), etched copper with residual errors, maker unknown, probably United States, *c.* second half of 19th century. Actual size.

by edge guides (figure 21). Edges were often crimped or folded to prevent the thin metal from bending, warping or curling.

The manufacture of stencils by etching probably declined in the first half of the twentieth century as the letters and monograms made so effectively by this method fell gradually out of fashion, and as other methods of manufacture were refined or developed. Etched stencils were, however, produced after 1950 in the German Democratic Republic and possibly elsewhere too, and they might still be found today.

Punching

The examples in the preceding section demonstrate that etching made possible stencil letters of almost any shape or size, and some of spectacular delicacy and detail. But neither etching nor cutting were always appropriate for stencil-making. Etching required knowledge of chemical processes and special facilities for them while cutting, at least at small sizes, demanded proficient handwork. Acquiring the necessary skills and techniques may have proved troublesome for many who wished to supply stencils; and stencils so made might be expensive in the time required to make them and thus in the price buyers had to pay. An alternative method of manufacture that resolves issues both of skill and cost is punching. Punching a letter from a blank plate is simpler than etching or cutting: to strike a punch cleanly, accurately and with consistency is the only significant manual skill required. And from its earliest mention as a method of manufacture, punching is indeed assumed to reduce the costs of production, an assumption demonstrated in later stencil-makers' catalogues.

Early instances of punching as a method of stencil manufacture are found in the late seventeenth and eighteenth centuries and are associated with playing cards.[29] In so far as sources on the stencilling of letters and words are concerned, Des Billettes (*c.* 1700) makes no mention of punches, though Breitkopf (1801: 33) does. He describes the work of Malo, father and son, of Paris who made stencil letters in a range of sizes, some as small as *cicero* (*c.* 12 point). Although Breitkopf had been told the stencils were 'pierced by hand', he writes that 'the evenness of the letters and the modest price [of the stencils] make one suspect that they are struck with sharp steel punches.' Breitkopf does not follow up his suspicion, but that he mentions punching at all suggests the method had some currency. Oddly, the *etched* stencils of Bery already described confirm the use of punches. In those with decorated letters (see figure 12b), small dot motifs show a ridge, or bur, on the underside of the plate where a punch was driven through it to form the dot; it allows punching to be identified with some certainty. This is the only part of Bery's letter where evidence of a punch is found, though one may have also made the inter-character spacing dot found to the right of small (i.e. lowercase) letters in some founts (figure 12, c–d).[30]

Since these instances of punching are ambiguous or indicate only a secondary role for the punch itself, uncertainty remains about just when and how an entire letter was cut in this way. It might be that some of the skills were borrowed, if not from the playing card maker, then from the typefounder for whom letter punches were indispensable and so considerably refined; or from artisans in other trades – gold- and silversmiths, medalists and bookbinders – who also made use of letter punches.[31] But to suggest that stencil-makers turned to others for

29. For example Des Billettes (*c.* 1700), Duhamel du Monceau (1762) and Diderot and D'Alembert (1751, etc.). Des Billettes' text includes a section titled 'Printing of playing cards' that describes punches carrying the four suit-signs. These were used to cut stencils of oiled canvas for printing the number, or point, cards (*les cartes de points*) and as illustrated in an engraving by Simonneau, dated 1697, they are flat-faced. Duhamel du Monceau, the general editor of the *Description des arts et métiers* as published from 1761, wrote the fascicule 'Art du cartier' (1762) which was accompanied by five engravings including Simonneau's of 1697 (plate II), now corrected by Patte. Duhamel du Monceau briefly describes the suit-sign punches as made of steel with a sharp cutting edge; they are, however, unaltered in the corrected engraving. In Diderot and D'Alembert's *Encyclopédie*, plate VI of the engravings illustrating the article 'Cartier'

includes suit-sign punches; these are shown with a raised cutting edge or outline. Other trades that used similar punches (though not for stencils) include faux flower-making, and fabric cutting and goffering. Each source given above (despite differences in the engravings) employs the term *emporte-pièce*, a punch designed for cutting out.

30. Bery's punch (or punches) may be associated with etching tools. Hind (1963: 2(8b.),

11) illustrates and describes a 'ring-punch' whose tip was circular and hollow; it was also used by goldsmiths. A ring-punch would easily produce the dots found in Bery's work, while the cutting edge around its hollow tip would help free the struck metal from the plate.

31. cf. Smeijers (1996: 58–62) where letter punches made by several trades are discussed.

guidance in cutting punches is to assume that they did not already possess the necessary skills themselves. Bery's own description on his trade card as a 'maker of letters in brass & steel' (*faiseur de caracteres en cuivre & en acier*) indicates that his work was not confined to stencil-making but possibly extended to engraving and punchcutting, and could imply a lateral application of techniques among his various activities. And if the punches that embossed the maker's marks onto Bery's stencils (see figure 12d) were by his own hand, then the genesis of punches for cutting stencil letters would only be a short conceptual leap away.

Despite these intimations of punching in Europe,[32] it is some decades later in North America that the earliest incontrovertible instances have so far been found. In 1860, Adoniram Judson Fullam established the American Stencil Tool Works in Springfield, Vermont where for the next ten years he manufactured punches for making stencils.[33] In a broadsheet of 1865, Fullam advertised two founts of punches: a large size (1 inch/*c.*25mm) carrying sans serif letters, numerals and basic punctuation (figure 22); and a smaller size whose dimensions and style are not stated or illustrated.[34] Another manufacturer, S. M. Spencer, was also in business in Brattleboro, about 30 miles to the south of Springfield and he, like Fullam, supplied punches, probably in several sizes.[35] Their primary customers were not, it appears, already-established stencil-makers but businesses who needed to regularly generate their own stencils, or enterprising individuals who, though largely or entirely inexperienced in stencil-making, were encouraged to pursue such work that – with punches – required little training or skill but promised decent returns. Fullam, for example, provided a lengthy justification for an investment in his punches and a roster of happy customers who had profited thereby. Punches thus functioned as an easy-to-use tool whose pre-formed letters enabled non-specialists to produce competent stencils, and whose manufacture enriched entrepreneurs who recognised the value in promoting and supplying equipment for what was, in essence, a species of do-it-yourself lettering.[36]

The letters carried by nineteenth-century stencil punches such as those sold by Fullam and Spencer are generally simple and robust in

Figure 22. Stencil letters carried by punches, from advertising broadsheet of Adoniram J. Fullam, American Stencil Tool Works, 1865. Actual size.
Courtesy of Special Collections, University of Vermont.

32. One additional early reference to punching stencils is, though ambiguous, worth noting. In a letter of 1811 to the *Journal of Natural Philosophy, Chemistry and the Arts*, G. Cumberland describes a stencil press devised by the English surgeon James Lind (1738–1812). Cumberland goes on to propose the reproduction of texts using stencils made thus: 'Let us suppose … a kind of copper or brass latten to be rolled thin for the purpose, and the writer to use a very corrosive ink, which in short time would cut quite through the whole body. He would by this means produce a stencil as fast as he could write, by means of which he would be enabled to print the right way. Again let us suppose he were to make use of capital letters only, acting as punches on paper, he would by this method have a paper stencil, that would last as long, perhaps longer, than the latten one … common ingenuity might overcome the difficulties of O and other letters by ties.' Quoted in Rhodes and Streeter (1999: 128–9).

33. Kebabian (1978).

34. Adoniram Judson Fullam, 'Dear Sir:– I take pleasure in calling your attention to my recently invented patent Stencil Dies …', Springfield, Vermont: American Stencil Tool Works, 1865 (Special Collections, Bailey/Howe Library, The University of Vermont). While one might conclude from Fullam's opening address that he invented stencil letter punches, the text of the patent

referred to (Adoniram J. Fullam, 'Punch', letters patent no. 27,793, 10 April 1860, Washington, D.C.: Unites States Patent Office) makes it clear that such punches were already known to him. Note that in North America 'punch' and 'die' are often used interchangeably, though among nineteenth-century manufacturers of stencils and related equipment the latter term was more common.

35. S .M. Spencer, 'Stencil Work!' (advertising circular), Brattleboro, Vermont, *c.* 1860–80 (Special Collections, Bailey/Howe Library, The University of Vermont, reproduced in Kindel (2002); letter from Helen A. Cunningham to her brother Henry E. Blake, April 17, 1866 (Manuscript File, Special Collections, Bailey/Howe Library, The University of Vermont) complaining of a failed transaction with Fullam and stating her optimism that Spencer was a more rep-

utable supplier; and Spencer (*c.* 1890) which illustrates the wide range of punches he offered after transferring his operations to Boston.

36. For Fullam and Spencer, an essential dimension of stencil letter punches was their portability and both clearly intended that they be used for canvassing. Fullam considered visits to farms an especially good means of generating business, while Spencer's advertising circular 'Stencil Work!' could be customized to announce the arrival of a travelling stencil-maker in town. Some of the earliest confirmed examples of punched stencils are name-plates made during the American Civil War (1861–5) for soldiers of the US (i.e. Union) Army of the northern states. They were used to mark a soldier's name and regimental designation onto clothes and equipment and could be acquired from sutlers and pedlars servicing army encampments.

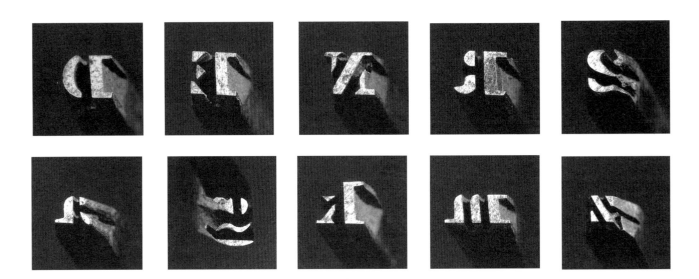

Figure 23. Stencil punches, steel, probably manufactured by S.M. Spencer, United States, *c.* 1860–1900. Capital height: 3 mm.

form, serifless or with slab serifs. This is true of both large- and small-size letters, although the latter are in some instances quite unconventional (figure 23), the result of several inter-related factors that are especially characteristic of punching.[37] While in the context of punching, large-size letters suffer few restrictions – their breaks do not drastically alter legibility and the size of the punch makes it sufficiently strong – small-size letters, and the punches that carry them, are subject to degradations in legibility and strength that are increasingly critical as size decreases. Strategies to counter these degradations may be largely responsible for the form of the letter. To demonstrate this, it is helpful to envision the entire work of punching small-size letters. When a stencil is cut with punches, each letter is struck anew, whenever it is called for. Punches are hammered repeatedly through the metal plate into a wood support beneath.[38] To withstand this, a sturdy punch is needed. At small sizes, sturdiness is particularly dependent on the resilience of the letterform cut on the punch. But other concerns also require attention. Like the punch, the stencil it generates must also be durable, and this too depends on the form of the letter. Wide breaks within the letter (as punch) should translate into wide and strong bridges in the stencil. Only then is the stencil best able to withstand the pressures its use will entail. But there are the demands of legibility as well. Now punch and stencil strength must be balanced against the tendency of stencil letters to become illegible as their size decreases. Details essential to the identity of a letter – proportion, counter size and shape, stem and curve thickness, and so on – must each remain expressive as the impulse to simplify form and provide suitably robust bridges push such details toward greater ambiguity.

Thus several complementary factors probably explain the particular forms of some small-size stencil letter punches, forms that are, simultaneously, an instructive demonstration in the coordination of form and function. But compelling though such coordination may be as an explanation, there is one further aspect of punch production that may be involved. According to Kebabian, Fullam trained as a machinist in the 1850s and was busy developing his punches at that time.[39] His patent of 1860, presumably an outcome of the work, specifies the use of

37. The observations that follow generally refer to serifless letters or those with slab serifs whose capital height is 1/4 inch (*c.* 6.4 mm) or less; the capital height of letters carried by stencil punches typically ranged from 3/32 inch (*c.* 2.4 mm) to at least 1 inch (*c.* 25.4 mm), though Spencer (*c.* 1890) states that punches carrying letters of any size or design could be made to order.

38. For this purpose Spencer (*c.* 1890) sold blocks of lignum vitae, a hard dense oily timber from trees of the genus *Guaiacum* native to the American tropics.

39. Kebabian (1978).

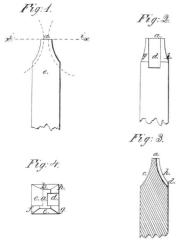

Figure 24. Adoniram J. Fullam, illustrations appended to 'Punch', letters patent no. 27,793, 10 April 1860.

Figure 25. Stencil, punched brass, from the set of G.W. Kinnan, United States, *c.* 1860–1900. Actual size. Front (top), and back showing lead stiffening frame.

Figure 26. Stencil, punched 'German silver' (nickel silver), United States, *c.* second half 19th century. Actual size.

a grinding wheel to produce a punch capable of cutting a (metal) stencil without leaving an underside bur (figure 24). Though the efficacy of this particular invention is uncertain, Fullam's grinding wheel would generate repeating forms throughout a fount of punches. And indeed straight and squared-off forms of the same dimension recur in the serifs and stems of Spencer's punches (none of Fullam's punches are presently known), as well as incisions of similar width. If these attributes are evidence of the machine tools used to cut the punches, then the forms of the letters they carry may also be assigned in part to their process of manufacture.

Among nineteenth-century stencils, those made by punching can usually be detected by the form of the letters used, by characteristic irregularities in letter- and word-spacing, misalignments and awkward arrangements of matter, and by underside burs (figure 25). While the quality of design and manufacture of some is decidedly mixed, many show considerable precision and a high standard of finish (figure 26), particularly in the alignment of consecutively struck punches and in the flattening and folding of the metal plate around its lead or zinc stiffening frame. By the early 1870s, one Philadelphia manufacturer who specialized in personal name-plates boasted 'the latest improvements in dies and machinery' (Quaker City Stencil Works, *c.* 1871) suggesting advances in punch design and working methods. At about this time too (though possibly earlier), letter punches appear with cutting

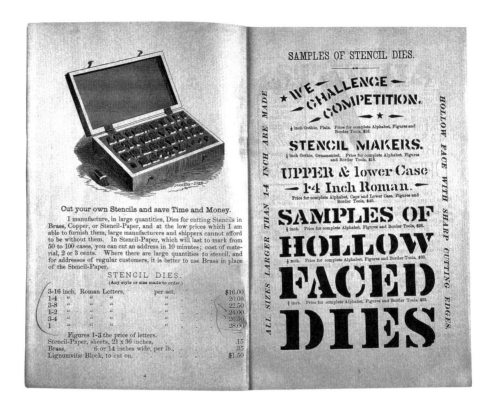

Figure 27. Stencil punches (dies) with cutting edges; and stencil letters available as punches. From S.M. Spencer (*c.* 1890).

a   *b*

c

Figure 28. Stencils, punched
a. oil-board (Reeves, UK)
b. aluminium (maker unknown, France)
c. celluloid (Econosign, UK)

40. Andrew J. Bradley, 'Stencil-machine', letters patent no. 494, 546, 4 April 1893, Washington, D.C.: United States Patent Office; and subsequent patents by others; see also Kindel (2001).

edges similar to those exploited by playing card makers (figure 27). In the 1890s, improvements in stencil punching were consolidated and reconfigured in a new patent invention: the stencil machine.[40] It struck well-formed and precisely aligned stencil letters from cardboard or oil-board and could, appropriately, be operated by workers with no stencil-making skills whatsoever. Whether by hand or machine, punching certainly resulted in cheaper stencils. Both Quaker City Stencil Works (*c.* 1871) and Quint (*c.* 1887–95) list the price of some as a third or a half less than others whose overall complexity was not significantly greater. The method of manufacture probably explains the difference: stencils with punched letters were less expensive than those with roundhands and broken-scripts whose finer forms required 'engraving' (probably etching). Stencil machines, of course, allowed stencils to be generated at almost no expense save the cost of the machine and the board it punched.

Stencil-making with punches (in the form of mechanical die-cutting and stamping) continues to the present day in a number of mass manufacturing contexts, though manual punching must be rare, if not defunct. Punched stencils are made of the usual materials of the nineteenth century including brass, zinc, tin, cardboard and oilboard (figure 28a) but also of aluminium, celluloid and plastic (figure 28, b-c), materials introduced in the twentieth century.

Miscellaneous

In addition to cutting, etching and punching, there are several other methods of manufacture that merit a brief description. They were probably all developed in the twentieth century and vary in sophistication. In some cases, the method contributes to the form of the letters, in others it does not.

Figure 29. Stencil, routed zinc, Italy, late 20th century. Reduced to 85 per cent linear.

Figure 30. Stencil, cut/folded/soldered, copper and wire, United States, *c.* late 19th/early 20th century. Reduced to 17 per cent linear.

Routing employs a rotating cutting head guided pantographically by a master letter pattern, or a pattern of letters and other graphic elements combined. The process is analogous to pantographic cutting used in the production of metal and wood printing types, though for stencil-making the rotating head cuts fully through the plate (figure 29). The router head may determine some attributes of form – including an occasion slip from the pattern that breaks the outline of the letter – though not the overall design. While the method is suitable for mass manufacture, it is ideal for producing letters of a quite specific size since adjustments to the pantograph's armature make possible a wide and continuous range of sizes. Routing is commonly used to cut stencils made of aluminium, tin, zinc and plastic. Other methods associated with plastic stencils include various kinds of moulding. These do not in themselves influence form in any noticeable way though the transparency of plastic encourages its use for stencils whose letters are made up of two or more parts. Recently, lasers have been configured for stencil-cutting, commonly with paper or card. Their precision is so great that despite the relative weakness of the material, the complex forms they can render match or surpass any produced by other methods. Stencils made in this way often remain as cut, that is to say, they become decorative objects and are not used for stencilling. Further methods of stencil-making – perhaps a great many – may also be located, some the result of circumstances where expediency and invention are fused to create forms unlikely to arise otherwise (figure 30).

Use

Having considered how the form of a stencil letter is influenced by the various tools and processes employed in its manufacture, similar consideration should be given to how its form is conditioned by the actual activity of stencilling. Of interest here is not only the apparently straightforward procedure by which a letter is stencilled onto some surface, but also those strategies that anticipate the work and their effect on the letter's final form.

Stencilling basics

The tools and materials associated with stencilling, apart from the
stencil itself, are relatively few. They include the brush (flat and round
rather than pointed) or other implements (a sponge, for instance, or a
spray can) used to apply ink or paint, the substrate that receives the ink
or paint, and any additional tools used to amend or embellish the form
of a letter once it has been stencilled. When stencilling letters, the form
the letter takes is partly determined by the characteristics of these tools
and materials. For instance, stencilled letters are rarely unmodulated;
instead, variations occur within or around the form of the letter. The
variations have little or nothing to do with the stencil but are instead
produced by the techniques used to apply the letter, and the nature of
the ink. Brushes or other ink- or paint-bearing tools may have some
influence: a stippling brush, a sponge or spray paint can produce a
number of textures; or spray paint may produce irregular edges if it
spreads beneath the stencil. Similarly, the ink or paint transparency,
opacity or viscosity may create further effects.[41] Substrates too play
a role when their unevenness or texture alters the form of the letter.
And after the letter has been marked out, the stenciller may amend
its breaks with a brush or pen, or embellish it with embroidery.

Compensations: thinning

Attributes of form, then, will arise through individual practices and
the use of various tools and materials during and after stencilling.
Those practices mentioned above are only suggestive of many others
that can enrich the stencilled letter. But it is also instructive to consider
strategies of design and manufacture that may anticipate the work of
stencilling and compensate for its technical characteristics by adjusting
the form of the letter in advance.

It has been argued (e.g. Smeijers, 1996: 121–2) that in the past (and
presently) the producers of printing types – punchcutters, designers
and manufacturers – foresaw how the types they were creating would
appear when printed. In anticipation, compensations were introduced
to counter degradations in form caused by how the type was generated
or manufactured, and how it behaved during printing. These compensations might, for instance, include 'traps' able to accommodate excess
ink captured at a typeform's junctions and angle apexes; or additional
or exaggerated elements able to buttress its corners and serifs. Overall,
the type as designed might be sharp and fine, even excessively thin, but
in the knowledge that subsequent processes of production and printing
would soften the form and add weight to it.

While it is uncertain that stencil-makers brought analogous compensations to the form of their letters in advance of stencilling, there
are good reasons why they might have done so. A letter well-cut from
a plate may seem a success: in negative, it looks well-formed and full.
But even if it is marked out accurately, in positive, it appears thinner.
This defect, evident in many stencilled letters, occurs because a dark
figure will usually appear smaller against a light ground than when the
figure-ground relationship is reversed. The thinness of the letter may
be exacerbated by its method of manufacture[42] or by the tools and
materials used to mark it out: a brush, for example, whose bristles are
insufficiently fine for the openings in the stencil, or ink whose thick-

41. The initials and large letters in
Thomas Bauer's liturgical books are stencilled with a thick opaque ink, almost in
an impasto manner, and rise up from the
substrate.
42. Among the several methods of manufacture, thinning often affects stencil letters cut with punches. When a flat-faced
punch is struck through a metal plate,
some metal is pushed out on the underside creating a flange that is later filed or
hammered flat. But in doing so, the size
of the cut out area may be reduced: the
flange is bent inward, closing up the forms
of the letter with attendant consequences
for marking out the letter.

ness causes it to accumulate in a stencil's corners. And these effects are
compounded by the very breaks of the stencil form that may simply
give the impression of a conventional letter imperfectly rendered.

So far there are no instances yet known of stencil-making conducted
with thinning in mind though Des Billettes intimates as much. While
the letter sizes he recommends and to some extent their form were
established by the size of the cutting and filing tools, he was also concerned that the letters be properly marked out. This was ensured if the
cut-out parts of the stencil were large enough to accommodate the
brush. But he does not go so far as to explicitly anticipate stencilling's
effect on the fullness of the letters. One senses that thinning was
understood by some stencil-makers, though not by all: a review of
eighteenth-century stencilled liturgical books shows substantial
variations in the weight of text letters; those that are fuller more convincingly counteract the visual wasting to which stencil letters are
susceptible. The work of Bauer (figure 16) is a salutary instance where
robust forms give his letters an uncommon strength and presence.

Compensations: multi-part letters

If it is difficult to demonstrate that compensations were consciously
devised to counteract the thinning of stencil letters, then another
scheme for configuring the final form of the letter is more certain, as it
constitutes a specific procedure to alter the letter as it is stencilled. As
mentioned, a stencil letter may be amended once it is marked out by
filling in its breaks with a brush or pen. This amendment is noteworthy
as it is a meagre solution to a worry that has long vexed stencillers: that
the breaks in the stencilled letter are evidence of an inferior or incor-
rect form. But a method of work exists that circumvents the difficulty.
It involves stencil letters that are split into two or more parts. The
parts are stencilled consecutively in a way that joins them together into
a complete letter. The breaks that would otherwise be visible in a
'normally' stencilled letter are thus disguised.

The importance of hiding the stencil letter's most typical attribute is
made plain by Des Billettes (*c.* 1700). His proposed method of work is
based on rendering the stencil letter without breaks, which he thought
'greatly disfigure[d] the beauty of this (kind of) printing'. Des Billettes
had considered filling in the breaks by hand, but imagined the stenciller would find this difficult or tedious and leave it undone, or decide
that the breaks were not in fact a defect. His proposal was to split in
two those letters that when cut as stencils would normally require
bridges. The two halves of the letter would be placed some distance
apart on the plate, with a 'guiding-mark' (*repère*) to the right of the first
half (figure 31; see also figures 5, 6). This guiding-mark, stencilled
along with the first half of the letter, would indicate the placement of
the second half and then be covered over when the second half was
stencilled. Des Billettes' proposal seems extreme at first since it
requires that stencil letters – already wilfully disjoined – be split apart
yet further on the plate, wherein the complete letter can no longer be
seen. But the underlying aim is hardly radical: to recompose the parts
into a single conventional entity.

Although ingenious, there is as yet little evidence that Des Billettes'
method of stencilling was commonly practised. But this is not to say

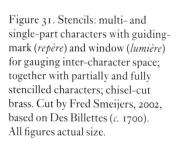

Figure 31. Stencils: multi- and
single-part characters with guiding-
mark (*repère*) and window (*lumière*)
for gauging inter-character space;
together with partially and fully
stencilled characters; chisel-cut
brass. Cut by Fred Smeijers, 2002,
based on Des Billettes (*c.* 1700).
All figures actual size.

that elements of it are absent from surviving artefacts. Guiding-marks, for instance, are found in eighteenth-century stencilled books: not for aligning parts of a letter, but for regulating distances between letters[43] (see figures 12, 16). Multi-part letters are also common, if usually reserved for large titles, initials, capital letters and similar instances where breaks are most obvious. Such letters, though split apart on the plate and rejoined when stencilled, were probably designed and deployed less programmatically than Des Billettes had specified. Breaks in the small letters in text are, by contrast, only rarely disguised. The work, it appears, was much too troublesome for most stencillers.[44]

Based on Des Billettes' proposal, and on subsequent uses of multi-part letters, it is probable that for many early stencillers the effort to disguise the stencil letter's technical origin was worthwhile if works of greater beauty and esteem were the result. Certainly in liturgical books of the grandest order they are used extensively and consistently. Some letters are of such fluency – that is to say, the breaks have been so cleverly and comprehensively hidden – that they at first resist an attribution of stencilling. Such works imply that in the context of worship at least, and in the production of books whose purpose was to elevate the expression of faith, little should intrude on the form of the letter that might suggest a method of making that was anything less than a full measure of devotion. Sievers (1825: 356) echoes this by quoting a maxim of the Papal Chapel, that 'music well written is already half sung' (*che musica ben scritta è mezza cantata*). This, he asserts, constituted a working principle of the scriptorium and it quite possibly applied to the (stencil) letters as well. But not all stencillers were so dutiful: in some liturgical books are found letters whose forms are entirely unamended. Boddeart, for instance, in his 'Graduale' makes few if any exertions to disguise breaks even among his largest titles and initials, though his efforts were clearly inspired. Perhaps he gloried in the stencil form – his dedication emphasizes how he made the book – free from the anxiety that his letters were in any way unworthy.

Beyond the context of faith and worship, stencil letters probably provoked less worry or concern as their applications widened. While few early artefacts other than books are presently known, Bery's specimen sheet (see figure 11) suggests a more relaxed and functional view of the stencil form. Among all his roman and italic letters, there is no effort to disguise the breaks, nor does the well-resolved design of his large capitals imply that their parts should be joined by the stenciller.[45] Moreover, though Bery advertises his work with a rather generic ecclesiastical reference, using *Eglise* (Church) as the specimen word, the devotion to 'good' form it might imply is absent. Instead, the reference is probably a convenient link to a context many already associated with stencil letters. Indeed, the numerous letter sizes he offers – far more than required for a liturgical book – and his efficient method of manufacture may well indicate his wish to supply a clientele whose applications for stencil letters were also secular and utilitarian. Perhaps for many or even most of his customers, the breaks of the stencil letter were either not thought disfiguring or were simply irrelevant.

By the second quarter of the nineteenth century, the use of stencil letters for making liturgical books was mostly abandoned[46] and so too

43. Comments made by Des Billettes indicate that such guiding-marks (*le point a costé de chaque lettre pour marquer les eloignements*) were in use when he was writing.

44. The sole example so far discovered in which all the breaks – in titles, large initials and text – are disguised is a French liturgical book of the early nineteenth century ('Les vespers de Notre Dame pendent l'avent', The Newberry Library: Wing MS 2Y 74651.6). Its letters are stencilled with exceptional precision: no spacing or alignment apparatus of any kind is visible and breaks are disguised using multi-part letters and occasional rubrications.

45. It might, however, be argued that disguising the breaks would obscure the kind of letter the specimen sheet displays.

46. This assertion is based on a lack of examples after the 1820s; on Sievers (1825: 357), who reports that stencilling had fallen into disuse sometime before his visit to the Papal Chapel; and on Rosenberg (1973: 83), who writes that the stencilling of books in the Mainz region ended when monasteries there were disbanded at the start of the nineteenth century.

Figure 32. Multi-part letters (right),
and an apparatus with two hinged
frames (labelled A and B above) for
stencilling them. From Hunter
(1946).

efforts to conceal the stencil form. But where multi-part stencil letters
are generally absent from rest of the nineteenth century, they re-
emerge in the twentieth in the work of signwriters. Hunter (1946),
describing professional practices stretching back nearly fifty years,
records a method of constructing multi-part letters and illustrates an
apparatus for stencilling them (figure 32). Other signwriters who were
stencillers may have adopted similar strategies, if not necessarily the
same equipment. Elsewhere, do-it-yourself signwriting sets such as
Econosign and Stencillor were also based on multi-part letters.[47] In
some respects, signwriting as devised by these sets resembles liturgical
book stencilling: since the letters supplied were often large, their
breaks would be obvious if left undisguised. Multi-part letters resolved
this failing. By doing so, the sets enabled shop owners to produce signs
of greater finesse and formality, even if the objects of worship thus
advertised were rather different from those of earlier centuries.

   Multi-part stencil letters are still used today, mostly in plastic
lettering guides; for stencilling proper, they are uncommon.

Design

It is plain from discussions so far that the form of a stencil letter is
closely linked to how and with what it is made, how it should perform
and what it should look like once stencilled. But form is not determined by these factors alone. Rather, an additional factor of design –
as noun and as verb – also accounts for much. To make clear the nature
of design's contribution to the stencil letter, the discussion that follows
is divided into two broad strands: adaptive and natural form.

Adaptive form

Many stencil letters are apparently derivative, that is to say they resemble models already established in other spheres of letter design but,
through subtle or obvious alterations, are adapted to the technical
requirements of stencilling. Des Billettes (*c.* 1700) again provides early
evidence. When describing stencilling, and thereafter the letters the
stenciller should cut, printing and printing types are his paradigm. He
ruminates on whether stencilling is more akin to writing or printing:

47. For users of Econosign, coordinating
the parts of the letter was simplified by
stencils made of transparent celluloid.

'one might … affiliate the art to that of the writer or scribe, as one could as aptly call it [a] scribing process as a printing process[;] but by the same token one could equally well affiliate it to printing: we decided rather more readily to do the latter owing to the specific affinity which exists between it and printing, inasmuch as both employ metal characters instead of a quill [pen].' When Des Billettes refers to the letters required, he states: 'one can distinguish the alphabets by sizes as in printing' and he mentions *gros parangon* and *gros canon*. Similarly, in describing the group of letters, he falls back on the typographical terms 'lowercase' and 'capitals' (*courante et sa majuscule, qui est justement / precisement ce que nous avons nommé dans l'imprimerie le bas de casse, et les capitales*). His measures to disguise the disfiguring breaks of the stencil letter may be taken as simply reinstating the original form of the letters, but they might also be construed as better enabling the stencilled letter to emulate the specific conventions of printing types. And in its entirety, Des Billettes's proposal is based on order and regularity. It de-emphasises skills that rely too heavily on manual fluency and coordination ('eye-balling') and replaces these with repeatable actions that are predetermined by the design and dimensions of the stencils and the equipment used with them.

Such qualities of a suggestively typographic kind are also evident in artefacts, books especially. There, stencil letters are combined in an organised manner to mark out text over many pages, as well as titles and initials. Letter sizes may bear a clear functional relationship to each other and within schemes of modular page construction that integrate musical notation and decorative matter (e.g. figure 16). There is in this an indication that some pre-existing typographic idiom has been adopted. Sievers (1825: 357), in describing the production or replacement of chants (probably in choirbooks), appears to allude to printing as the default model: 'The present scribes of the Papal Chapel have given up this mechanical-artistic method of copying [i.e. stencilling] and write with a pen. Their copies are, it is true, also excellent, and better than one could imagine without having seen them; but without the degree of symmetry that the old copying method produces'. One cannot be certain that printing preceded the stencilling, but 'the degree of symmetry' could imply this. Elsewhere, an *Antiphonarium* demonstrates these practices: most of it is printed with types, but bound in are several stencilled sections and, subsequently, additional handwritten sections.[48]

If it can be established by general comparison and, in a few instances by specific practice, that printing was a model for stencilling, then it follows that some stencil letters were derived from printing types. But while intimations abound, direct connections are fleeting. Des Billettes (*c.* 1700) offers no advice on the models a stencil-maker might follow, suggesting only that letters should be beautifully proportioned and 'the letters one wants to cut'. Stencilled letters in liturgical books usu-

48. *Antiphonarium*, 1614, Gilmore Music Library, Yale University, New Haven. It is probable, judging from the form of the letters used, that the stencilled sections were added in the 18th century. Similar additions are found in printed liturgical books from the Mainz region (Gottron, 1938). While the present discussion emphazises the affinity of stencilling and printing, it is worthwhile to note the features stencilled books often share with manuscripts. They include substrate (vellum), techniques of page layout (pinpricks to mark line ends, scoring to mark baselines and other delineations) and illumination (applications of multi-coloured decoration).

dér R egl R

a   *b*

gaed B B gaud D R Æ

c   *d*

Figure 33. Adaptive form.
a. unidentified liturgical book fragment, Gilmore Music Library, Yale
   University
b. Bery, no. 5, *c.* 1781; cf. figure 11
c. Bauer, *c.* 1760; cf. figure 16
d. unidentified liturgical book fragment, Gilmore Music Library, Yale
   University
All examples reproduced actual size
from sources given.

ally follow the roman model as would be natural in the Roman Catholic
context from which most of these books emanated. The letters are,
however, only generally roman: while they echo the attributes of large-
size missal or choral types, they often exhibit lively idiosyncrasies
(figure 33). A stencil-maker's process of work might be the cause:
existing letters and types would provide a starting point, but these
would pass through a filter of aesthetic pre-dispositions, technical
ingenuity or incompetence, and some or little understanding of the
conventionally well-formed roman letter. The letters so generated
would be distinctly typographic but with irregular or eccentric attributes, their design not bluntly adaptive – the model left untouched save
the abrupt introduction of breaks – but rather more knowingly or
unwittingly mediated.

Many stencil letters fall within this description, very like printing
types but difficult to link to a specific model. Bery's letters are redolent
of offerings from contemporary French and Dutch typefoundries
though no precise matches are observed. But aligning stencil letters
too closely with printing types may be unwise in some cases: to take
Bery again, his larger decorated capitals and *bâtardes* are detailed and
flourished to a degree rarely seen in printing types; the exuberance of
the *bâtardes*, in particular, is more readily associated with the writing
master and the engraver. And as the applications for stencil letters
widened, especially into commercial ephemera – as much the domain
of the engraver (and later the lithographer) as the letterpress printer –
no doubt the models that guided stencil-makers grew in number. Early
nineteenth-century stencilled bookplates suggest this while among
later stencilled monograms, visiting cards, labels and billheads, letter
styles and forms recognisable from engraving, lithography and printing are all in evidence. Borrowing from a variety of models would be
even more likely if stencil-making was only one of several services
offered by individuals or companies who also worked in other lettering
media.

Among stencil letters made since the nineteenth century, adaptive
form remains the dominant mode. In general, the impulse to adapt

may simply be a matter of convenience, efficiency and habit. But an adaptation may also be a practical reaction to the exigencies of style and fashion dictated from elsewhere, a demonstration that stencilling is a viable and up-to-date alternative to other species of lettering and printing.

Natural form

Stencil letters of natural form are distinct from those that are adaptive in that their contiguity of ground is fundamental to their overall conception rather than imposed on an existing model: the design is 'natural' to the demands of stencil-making.[49] Natural form in this sense is first apparent when breaks are coherently integrated into an existing letter that was originally unbroken. The stencil letter remains essentially adaptive, though the intention is a design that is technically appropriate but not obviously so. Thereafter, an attribution of natural form is increasingly apt as the effects of adaptation disappear or elude detection and fully appropriate when adaptation is irrelevant as a description. Natural form may also be assigned a supplementary feature that adds considerable interest to it: genesis within the work of stencilling. Many letters are made for stencilling but most are adaptive; those that are natural stencil forms *and* designed specifically for stencilling are far less common. While the identification of natural stencil letters made wholly for stencilling will in many cases prove inconclusive, their existence, if established, may illustrate instances where the work of stencilling has made an original contribution to the broader sphere of letter design.

Because decoration and pattern-making – whether on walls, furniture, fabrics, or in books – is often constructed of unjoined elements (i.e. on a contiguous ground), natural stencil letters are encouraged in contexts where they join with decorative inventions. The connection between decoration and stencil letters must be significantly old; again, Des Billettes (*c.* 1700) is the earliest explicit reference: 'in order to ornament this kind of printing [i.e. stencilling] one can also make all sorts of characters bearing fleurons, vignettes, cartouches, etc. which are used in printing, whether to mark them out in one go, in one colour alone, or else to make the outline only, and then illuminate it in different colours with a paintbrush'. Here, decoration embellishes the artefact to which (adaptive) stencil letters also contribute, but the forms of each are independent. This is true of many stencilled books that incorporate decoration.

Less frequent is decoration that builds the letter in its entirety to produce natural stencil letters. The earliest examples so far discovered occur in Boddeart's work (figures 34a, 14). His letters are constructed of straight and curving stems sprouting (rose) thorns and tendrils that bi- and trifurcate at their extremities; they are not merely embellished, they are pure decoration. While the style of Boddeart's work echoes that of contemporary engravers and typefounders, his letters are natural and apparently indigenous to stencilling. Similar letters are found in the following decades in France including Bery's, whose sinuous decorated capitals (figure 34c) are natural stencil forms of great complexity. Thereafter, no similar examples have been located until the middle decades of the nineteenth century, when decorated stencil

49. Natural form refers only to stencil letters that are a single entity with contiguous ground, and not multi-part letters or other exceptions given in note 5.

a. Boddeart (1755); cf. figure 14
b. unidentified liturgical book fragment,
   Gilmore Music Library, Yale University
c. Bery (c. 1781); cf. figures 11 & 12b

d. maker unknown, c. mid 19th century,
   probably Britain
e. Quint (c. 1887–95)
f. maker unknown, c. 2nd half 19th century,
   probably United States
g. maker unknown, c. 2nd half 19th century,
   probably Germany
h. maker unknown, c. 2nd half 19th century,
   Germany

i.–j. Johann Merkenthaler, from an
   advertising circular, c. 1900, Germany
k. Georges Auriol, c. 1900, France
l. Josef Albers, 'Schablonenschrift',
   c. 1923–26, Germany
m. Econosign, from advertising catalogue
   c. 1930s, Britain
n. Hunter (1946)

Figure 34. Natural form.
a–c, e, i–j, m–n: reproduced from
source given.
d, f–h: marked out from extant
stencil.
All examples reproduced actual size
except e, k, l and n.

letters recur in large numbers in England, Germany and North America (figure 34, d–g).[50] Some continuity exists between these nineteenth- century examples and their eighteenth-century forbears in the furcated terminals and mid-stem motifs; and many are shaded or otherwise three-dimensional in appearance with their breaks subtly resolved into the overall form of the letter. Late nineteenth- and early twentieth-century stencil letters designed as guides for needlework are also nearly natural in form and occasionally, as in 'cross-stitch' designs, are entirely so (figure 34i). But the specific source of their design remains outside stencilling.

Over the past one hundred years or so, other examples of natural stencil letters whose creation may be located within the work of stencilling occur only sporadically. Artists and designers working in the stylistic milieu of Art Nouveau and Jugenstil occasionally devised natural stencil letters to match other pictorial forms and patterns based on separate but fluidly integrated elements (figure 34, j–k). It is likely that some of this work was made for, or encouraged by stencilling, a popular means of decorating at the time. Letters designed along these lines are also found in contemporary lettering and type design compendia, and – suggestively – in stencilling and decorating manuals.[51] Among artists and designers of the modern movement, stencil letters were also of interest, partly for their associations with industry and engineering, but also for their open, constructed forms that aligned well with broader strategies of visual design. One iconic example is 'Schablonenschrift' (i.e. 'Stencil type'), an alphabet devised *c.* 1923–6 by Josef Albers purportedly for stencilling (figure 34l). The design is based around a few simple geometric elements that when variously configured produce an extreme, though still recognisable, rendition of conventional letters. But neither the process of design nor its outcome can be described as adaptive, making Albers' stencil letters largely natural.[52] Other examples leading up to the present day are not difficult to locate, but most are printing types or letters designed for specific (non-stencilling) commissions and may only use natural stencil forms for stylistic reasons. The association of individual designs with stencilling is usually problematic; if a link does exist, as in the case of stencilled signs or graffiti, the design itself may only be ephemeral.

Implications

This recollection of stencil letters suggests that beyond the examples discussed here is a yet larger narrative whose many parts remain unassembled. But by recollecting at least some of the story, the themes that characterize stencil letters come roughly into focus: design that is 'high' or 'low', sacred or vernacular; manufacture that is skilled or rude, mass or customized; applications that are base and functional or a hymn to glory; a technology that offers a mundanely practical kind of lettering or an alternative to printing that embraces the elaborate conceits of manuscript production. Among these themes and others, many matters beg further investigation: the impetus to reproduce texts with stencils, the details of ecclesiastical and commercial stencil-making practices, the evolution and expansion of stencil letter applications, the influences stencillers felt from other trades, and so on.

50. Few nineteenth-century stencil letters from France, decorated or otherwise, have yet been found and thus are not included in this essay; but they are likely to exist in some variety.

51. e.g. Scott-Mitchell (1906), Day (1914), and later Hunter (1946).

52. 'Schablonenschrift' warrants some additional comment as it is both related to later printing types (e.g. Futura Black, Transito, Braggadocio) and is a design that may itself draw on several stencil-related antecedents. Of these, the first occurs in propaganda posters executed by ROSTA artists in the Soviet Union between 1919 and 1922. There, natural stencil letters were constructed from simply cut forms and, as the posters were often stencilled, it is likely that the letters were invented with this use in mind. A second antecedent is found in paintings and graphic work executed by Fernand Léger immediately after the First World War where letters are used. Léger's appear to be an extreme simplification of a Didot-like modern face roman (or fat face), or of stencil letters adapted from them (numerous other artists and designers made subsequent use of such letters, again especially in the Soviet Union). Léger's own debt is probably to Cubist and Futurist painters who before and during the First World War used stencil letters in their paintings and drawings (Georges Braque apparently the first to do so). The particular stencil letter they chose was then and is still commonly used in many parts of Europe. See also Chatelain (1994). In regard to Albers' 'Schablonenschrift', it is interesting to observe that some stencil letters manufactured as punches (see figure 23) are uncannily similar, if less self-consciously unconventional.

At root, stencil letters are frequently disconcerting: convention
wilfully disintegrated, disfigured, debased and abstracted. Where its
compromises have been unacceptable, the stencil form has been disguised by procedures that return it to more familiar territory. But for
those who have seen in the stencil letter's necessary technical expression room for imaginative essays in design, its open figure and contiguous ground are the source of much ingenuity and, in a few instances,
truly inventive letters. Both approaches are discerned in artefacts and
accounts that survive, as are other approaches less doctrinaire or innovative, adopted through force of necessity using a technology of convenience. To draw together their fuller history, many more episodes of
stencil letters should be fixed. The few sketched out here give clues
for where to look next.

Acknowledgements

While assembling this essay, I enjoyed a warm welcome and much
valuable assistance from Richard Boursy at the Gilmore Music
Library, Yale University (New Haven); Sue Ann Prince, Rob Cox
and Claire Goldsteen at the American Philosophical Society
(Philadelphia); Annelen Ottermann and Frau Ripperger at the
Stadtbibliothek-Mainz; and Paul Gehl at The Newberry Library
(Chicago). I must also extend my gratitude to Veronica Heath, James
Mosley, Gillian Rose Knight, Richard Boursy and Nadja Guggi for
assistance with translations; Prudence Doherty at the Bailey/Howe
Library (The University of Vermont), Gladys Quint Wigfield and
Richard Wigfield for supplying information on nineteenth-century
stencil-making in North America; David Knott for supplying exam-
ples of stencilled bookplates and marks of ownership; Paul and Judy
Kindel for assistance in gathering artefacts in North America; Karl
and Carrol Kindel for research at the United States Patent and
Trademark Office; Michael Twyman, Paul Stiff, James Mosley and
Fred Smeijers for reading the essay in draft and suggesting numerous
improvements to it; Catherine Dixon and Margaret Smith for advice
on, respectively, the sections 'What is a stencil letter?' and 'Design';
Amoret Tanner and John Blatchly for lending artefacts in their collections; and my colleagues in the Department of Typography & Graphic
Communication for their unceasing supply of ideas and leads. Visits to
the American Philosophical Society and the Stadtbibliothek-Mainz,
work to reconstruct items described by Des Billettes, and the purchase
of images from various institutions were all made possible by a grant
from the Arts & Humanities Research Board (UK) awarded through its
'Small grants in the creative and performing arts' scheme. Stencilled
books in the collections of the Gilmore Music Library, the Stadtbibliothek-Mainz and The Newberry Library, and the engraving of
Simonneau in the collection of St Bride Printing Library are reproduced by permission. Items from the stencil set of Bery are reproduced
by permission of the American Philosophical Society. Extracts from
the MS of Des Billettes are quoted by permission of The Newberry
Library. Photography: figures 3, 6, 7–9, 19–21, 23, 25–8, 29–31 by
Media Services (The University of Reading); figure 12 by the author.

References

Abbe, Dorothy (ed.). 1980. *Stencilled ornament & illustration*, Boston: Trustees of the Boston Public Library

Bery. *c.* 1781.'Faiseur de caracteres pont Notre Dame', etc. (specimen sheet), Paris, Franklin Miscellaneous Collection B:F85.93, Library of the American Philosophical Society, Philadelphia

Blatchly, John. 2000. *Some Suffolk and Norfolk ex-libris: bookplates and labels relating to East Anglian owners, artists and printers*, London: The Bookplate Society

Bliss, Douglas Percy. 1930. 'The stencil process in France and England', *Penrose's Annual*, vol. 32, London: Percy Lund Humphries

Boddaert, U. 1755. 'Graduale Romanum de Tempore & Sanctus', Flanders: Abbey of Loo, Gilmore Music Library, Yale University, New Haven

Breitkopf, Johann Gottlob Immanuel. 1801. *Versuch, den Ursprung der Spielkarten, die Einführung des Leinenpapieres und den Anfang der Holzschneidekunst in Europa zu erforschen, Zweyter Theil, aus des Verfassers Nachlasse herausgegeben und mit einer Vorrede begleitet von Johann Christian Friedrich Roch*, Leipzig: Roch und Compagnie

Brignall, Colin and others. 1996. *Letraset & stencil cutting*, New York and London: International Typeface Corporation and St Bride Printing Library

Carr, Francis. 1961. *A guide to screen process printing*, London: Vista Books

Chatelain, Roger. 1994. 'Une police qui intrigue', *Revue Suisse de l'Imprimerie*, no. 6

Crouch, Howard R. 1995. *Civil war artifacts: a guide for the historian*, Fairfax, Virginia: SCS Publications

Day, Lewis F. 1914. *Lettering in ornament*, 2nd edn., London: Batsford

Des Billettes, Gilles Filleau. *c.* 1700.'Imprimerie de Livres d'Eglise, Escriteaux ou sentences &c.' and 'Imprimerie des cartes a Jeux', Case Wing MS +Z4029.225, The Newberry Library, Chicago

Diderot and D'Alembert (eds.). 1751, etc. *Encyclopédie, ou dictionnaire raisonné des sciences, des arts, et des métiers* and related plates, Paris

Duhamel du Monceau, Henri-Louis. 1761, etc. 'Art du cartier' (1762), fascicule of the *Description des arts et métiers*, Paris; collected in *Les arts du papier*, Geneva: Slatkine Reprints, 1994

Fischer von Waldheim, Gotthelf. 1800–4. 'Über ein in der Mainzer Universitätsbibliotheck befindliches durch Blech geschriebenes Chorbuch', *Beschreibung einiger typographischer Seltenheiten*, vol. 3, Mainz

Gottron, Adam. 1938. 'Beiträge zur Geschichte der kirchenmusikalischen Schablonendrucke in Mainz', *Gutenberg-Jahrbuch*, pp. 187–93

Heinecken, Karl Heinrich von. 1771. *Idée générale d'une Collection Complette d'Estampes*, Leipzig & Vienna: J.P. Kraus

Hind, Arthur Mayger. 1963 (1923). *A history of engraving & etching*, 3rd edn., New York: Dover Publications

Hoep, Karl. *c.* 1939. *Signier-Schablonen* (product catalogue), Leipzig: Sächsische Metall-Schablonen-Fabrik

Hunter, Alfred. 1946. *Professional ticket writing,* 2nd edn., London: Blandford Press

Hutchings, R. S. 1965. *A manual of decorated typefaces,* London: Cory, Adams & Mackay

Hutchings, R. S. 1958. 'Stencil types', *The British printer,* vol. 71, no. 10

Jammes, André. 1965. 'Académisme et typographie: the making of the romain du roi', *Journal of the Printing Historical Society,* no. 1

Jansen, Hendrik. 1808. *Essay sur l'origine de la Gravure en bois et en taille-douce, et sur la connaissance des estampes des XVe et XVIe siècles,* vol. 2, Paris: F. Schoell

Jones, J. *c.* 1885. Sample book of J. Jones, printer and engraver, Corn Market, Derby, Wing MS 35, The Newberry Library, Chicago.

Kebabian, Paul B. 1978. 'A.J. Fullam's American Stencil Tool Works', *The Chronicle,* vol. 31, no. 2, Early American Industries Association.

Kindel, Eric. 2001. 'Marked by time', *Eye,* vol. 10, no. 40

Kindel, Eric. 2002. 'Stencil work in America, 1850–1900', *Baseline,* no. 38

Kinross, Robin. 1986. 'What is a typeface?', *Baseline,* no. 7, republished in *Unjustified texts,* London: Hyphen Press, 2002

Lacroix, Paul. 1852. *Histoire de l'Imprimerie et des Arts et Professions qui se Rattachent à la Typographie,* Paris: Adolphe Delahays

Lingelbach, William E. 1948. 'B. Franklin, printer – new source materials', *Proceedings of the American Philosophical Society,* vol. 92, no. 2

Lord, Francis A. 1975. *Civil War collector's encyclopedia,* vol. 2, West Columbia, South Carolina: Lord Americana & Research

Mackenzie, F. W. 1950. 'The stencil', *The Penrose Annual,* London: Lund Humphries

Manco, Tristan. 2002. *Stencil graffiti,* London: Thames & Hudson

Marcus, Susan. 1972. 'The typographic element in Cubism, 1911–1915: its formal and sematic implications', *Visible Language,* vol. 6, no. 4

Marsh stencil (product catalogue). *c.* 1947. Belleville, Illinois: Marsh Stencil Machine Company

Merkenthaler, Johann. *c.* 1900. *Monogramme zur Wäsche-Stickerei* (product catalogue), Nürnberg: Johann Merkenthaler Metallschablonenfabrik

Miller, J. Abbott. 1993. 'Word art', *Eye,* vol. 3, no. 11

Montreal Stencil Works. 1927. *General catalogue,* no. 20, Montreal: Montreal Stencil Works

Mosley, James. 1997. 'French academicians and modern typography: designing new types in the 1690s', *Typography papers* 2

Mosley, James (ed.). 1995. The *Manuel typographique* of Pierre-Simon Fournier le jeune, together with *Fournier on typefounding,* an English translation of the text by Harry Carter, Darmstadt: Technische Hochschule

O'Meara, Eva Judd. 1933. 'Notes on stencilled choir-books', *Gutenberg-Jahrbuch,* pp. 169–85

Phillips, Stanley S. 1974. *Excavated artifacts from battlefields and campsites of the Civil War, 1861–1865,* Lanham, Maryland: privately printed

Proudfoot, W. B. 1972. *The origin of stencil duplicating*, London: Hutchison & Co.

Quint. *c.* 1887–95. *Quint's Stencil, Stamp, and Letter Works* (product catalogue), Philadelphia: S. H. Quint & Sons

Quaker City Stencil Works. *c.* 1871. *Illustrated circular of designs and price list of different methods of marking linen with indelible ink, stencil plates, stamps, pens, indelible pencils, etc.* (product catalogue), Philadelphia: Quaker City Stencil Works

Rhodes, Barbara J. and Streeter, William W. 1999. *The art and history of mechanical copying, 1780–1938*, New Castle, Delaware: Oak Knoll Press

Richford, E. M. *c.* 1920. *Richford's India rubber stamps, type pads &c.* (product catalogue), London: E. M. Richford

Rickards, Maurice. 2000. *The encyclopedia of ephemera* (Michael Twyman, ed.), London: The British Library

Rivard, Karen and Brinkmann, Thomas H. 1968. *The marking story: a history of marking & marking devices and of the marking industry in North America*, Chicago: Marking Device Association

Rodrigues, Alberto. 1973. 'Die Schablonendrucke des Paters Thomas Bauer in der Stadtbibliothek Mainz', *Gutenberg-Jahrbuch*, pp. 85–99

Rosenfeld, Hellmut. 1973. 'Der Gebrauch der Schablone für Schrift und Kunst seit der Antike und das schablonierte Buch des 18. Jahrhunderts', *Gutenberg-Jahrbuch* pp. 71–84

Russ, Stephen. 1969. *Practical screen printing*, London: Studio Vista

Saudé, Jean. 1925. *Traité d'enluminure d'art au pochoir*, Paris: Aux Éditions de l'Ibis

Schreiber, Heinrich. 1927. 'Thomas Bauer', *Die Bibliothek der ehemaligen Mainzer Karthause, die Handschriften und ihre Geschichte*, 60. Beiheft zum Zentralblatt für Bibliothekwesen, Leipzig: Otto Harrassowitz

Scott-Mitchell, Frederick. 1906. *Practical stencil work*, London: Trade Papers Publishing Company

Sievers, G. L. P. 1825. 'Die Päpstliche Kapelle zu Rom', *Allgemeine musikalische Zeitung*, no.22 (1 June)

Smeijers, Fred. 1996. *Counterpunch*, London: Hyphen Press

Spencer, S. M. *c.* 1890. *S.M. Spencer's stencil & rubber stamp works* (product catalogue), Boston: S.M. Spencer

Sylvia, Stephen W. and O'Donnell, Michael J. 1978. *The illustrated history of American Civil War relics*, Orange, Virginia: Moss Publications

Tomlinson, Charles (ed.). 1854. *Cyclopaedia of useful arts*, London & New York: George Virtue

The Wharton Novelty Co. *c.* late 19th century. *Brass stencils for marking show cards, boxes, bags, trunks, &c.* (product circular), Marysville, Ohio: The Wharton Novelty Co.

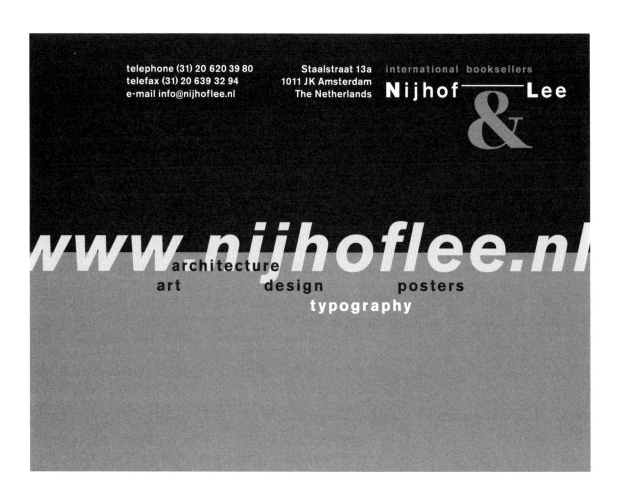

Ole Lund

The public debate on Jock Kinneir's road sign alphabet

There has been some recent interest in Jock Kinneir and Margaret Calvert's influential traffic signs and accompanying letterforms for Britain's national roads from the late 1950s and early 1960s. Their signs and alphabets prompted a unique public debate on letterform legibility, which provoked the Road Research Laboratory to carry out large-scale legibility experiments. Many people participated in the debate, in national newspapers, design and popular science magazines, technical journals, and radio. It was about alphabets and signs that would soon become – and still are – very prominent in Britain's 'visual landscape' and elsewhere in the world. The debate still surfaces occasionally, often with the facts severely distorted. This article, supported by studies of archival sources, traces the public debate.

author's address
Gjøvik University College
PO box 191
N-2802 Gjøvik
Norway
ole.lund@hig.no

Prelude

In August 1961 two researchers at the Road Research Laboratory in Britain published a paper on the 'Relative effectiveness of some letter types designed for use on road traffic signs' (Christie and Rutley 1961b). It appeared in the journal *Roads and Road Construction*. A shorter version was published in *Design* the same month (Christie and Rutley 1961c). These two papers were both based on a report 'not for publication' finished in January the same year (Christie and Rutley 1961a). These papers represented the culmination of a vigorous public debate on letterform legibility which had been going on since March 1959. The controversy and the Road Research Laboratory's subsequent experiments happened in connection with the introduction of direction signs for Britain's new motorways.[1]

The design of these directional and other informational motorway signs represented the first phase of an overall development of a new coherent system of traffic signs in Britain between 1957 and 1963. The new system was a late British adaptation to, but not an adoption of, European practice and the UN Geneva protocol of 1949. The new British system contained a large number of innovative direction signs for use on motorways (including direction signs on 'all-purpose' roads pointing to connected motorways), direction signs for use on major 'all-purpose' roads, and direction signs for use on local 'all-purpose' roads. The new British system also included basic categories of largely pictorial trafffic signs (both iconic and symbolic), such as mandatory signs, prohibitory signs and warning signs. Although modified and redrawn, the basic pictorial traffic signs were more directly adopted from the 1949 Geneva Protocol than were the direction signs.[2]

1. Motorways had been discussed in the Ministry of Transport since before the second world war (when they had been built in Germany, Italy and the USA). A working party was set up in 1953; it produced a general report (5 Feb. 1955). A short report on 'Signs for motorways' was produced in the Ministry (8 Nov. 1955). In 1957, after work had begun on the M1 (London – Birmingham) another report, 'Notes on motorway signs', came out. The Anderson committee on 'Motorway signs' was established in autumn 1957. The minister set up another committee, in order to advise on general road signs. (PRO: MT 126/1). Ideas of building motorways in Britain date back to the turn of the century; pressure increased from the mid 1930s (Charlesworth 1984; Smith 1998).

2. For background, see Moore and Christie 1960 (by two researchers at the Road Research Laboratory, comparing motorway direction signing in Britain, Germany and the USA); Schreiber 1961 (a history of roads); Spencer 1961 (an illustrated depiction of Britain's chaotic and insular traffic signs before this work started); Ministry of Transport 1962 (The 'Anderson report' on traffic signs for motorways); Ministry of Transport 1963 (The 'Worboys report' on traffic signs for 'all-purpose' roads); Froshaug 1963 (profusely and systematically illustrated article on the development of traffic signs and the Geneva 1949 protocol, leading up to the new British traffic sign system based on the recommendations of the Worboys committee); Ministry of Transport and Central Office of Information 1965 (leaflet presenting 'The new traffic signs'); Moore n.d.(review of legibility research on road direction signs); Krampen 1983 (a special issue of *Semiotica*, on the origin and development of road sign systems in an international context), Charlesworth 1984 (the prehistory and history of British motorways); Charlesworth 1987 (history of the Transport and Road Research Laboratory); Department of Transport 1991 (brief history of traffic signs in Britain); Department of Transport 1994 (design manual for British directional signs); Department of Transport 1995 (comprehensive exposition of current British traffic signs); Smith 1998 (prehistory and history of British motorways); Baines 1999 (richly illustrated article on the British 'Kinneir/Calvert' road signs).

3. Sir Colin Anderson (1904–1980) had a distinguished career in transport and was president, National Council of the Design and Industries Association 1950–53, member of the Council of Industrial Design 1951–60, chairman of the Contemporary Art Society 1956–60, chairman of the Orient Line 1952–60, director of Midland Bank 1950–74 (Moriarty 2000, p. 57).

4. Froshaug 1963, p. 50; also Krampen 1983, p. 110.

5. Kinneir (1917–94) trained as an engraver; after wartime active service he designed exhibitions for Central Office of Information. He joined Design Research Unit in 1950. He started a design practice in 1956; one of his first jobs was the signing system for Gatwick Airport. He had just completed a baggage labelling system for Sir Colin Anderson's Orient Line, when he was engaged as a designer for the Anderson committee. (Hopkins 1964; Stephenson 1971; Kinneir 1983; Kinross 1994).

6. See Kinneir 1970, pp. 15–16.

7. Margaret Calvert (b. 1936). 'In the studio, Margaret Calvert's eye for detail was crucial in the drawing of the alphabets and the pictorial signs.' (Baines 1999, p. 32).

8. 'We have as a committee got into the habit of accepting the general weight & appearance of the German alphabet as being the sort of things we need! I think therefore something on these lines is what the committee believes it wants.' Letter from Colin Anderson to Jock Kinneir, 26 June 1958. (Margaret Calvert, London).

9. Kinneir 1971, p. 6; 1984, p. 344.

10. The skeletal structure of several characters in Kinneir's alphabet (a, c, e, g, k, y, s) resembles another sans serif, the Berthold Grotesk. However, the latter has a quite different overall look.

11. Akzidenz Grotesk 'halbfett' was issued in 1909 by Berthold in Berlin (ATypI 1975, p. 1), as a member of its existing Akzidenz Grotesk family. The display of 'halbfette' Akzidens Grotesk in F. Bauer's comprehensive account of new typefaces issued in Germany 1908–1912 (Bauer 1912, p. 290), suggests that 1914 for 'halbfette' Akzidenz Grotesk in Seemann 1926 (p. 205) must be wrong. The Akzidenz Grotesk family was developed from sans serifs from the Bauer foundry in Stuttgart, which had been acquired by H. Berthold AG in 1897 (Bertheau 1995, pp. 2, 85, 92, 512–513, 558–559; Bauer 1928, pp. 25, 179).

12. Parallel to the continental popularity of Monotype's similar but somewhat more quirky Grotesque 215 and bold 216. (First issued 1926, and influenced by 19th century sans serifs from Stephenson Blake.)

13. The numerals for route numbers only (& letters A, B, and M) were designed differently from the main numerals for distances and later for numbering motorway exits: they are condensed and rather angular.

The motorway alphabet

The advisory committee on traffic signs for motorways (1957–1962), set up by the Ministry of Transport, and chaired by Sir Colin Anderson,[3] consulted a large number of interested organisations and it also did something which was then ground-breaking:[4] in June 1958 it appointed a professional designer. Jock Kinneir[5] had by then already designed the signing system for Gatwick Airport.[6] Together with his young assistant Margaret Calvert,[7] and on the basis of the committee's broad recommendations, he designed the elegant and innovative motorway direction signs, as well as their accompanying letterforms.

Kinneir, who had rejected on 'aesthetic grounds' the committee's initial wish[8] to employ the German DIN sans serif lettering of capitals and small letters,[9] designed a new sans serif alphabet (see figure 1). It resembles and was probably based on the typeface Akzidenz Grotesk from the German type foundry Berthold (see figure 2). Both Richard Hollis (1994, p. 161) and James Mosley (1999, p. 9) claim that Kinneir's alphabet for road and motorway signs was based on Akzidenz Grotesk, or Standard as it was called in English speaking countries. A careful visual inspection of Akzidenz Grotesk 'halbfett' (Standard 'medium') and semi-bold (not regular) variants of similar sans serif typefaces with open semi-enclosed counters and diagonally cut terminals of letters like a, c, e and s, supports this claim. That is, a strong family resemblance is present between Kinneir's alphabet and Akzidenz Grotesk 'halbfett', while the individual shape of several letters are different.[10] Thus, Kinneir's alphabet is far from a mere modification of Akzidenz Grotesk 'halbfett'. It is a unique alphabet with a combination of many specific features such as the discriminating Edward Johnston-like 'legibility' hook on the lower case letter l, the noticeable round dots of the lower case i and j, the diagonally cut terminal of the lower case letter a (unlike the inconsistent horizontally-cut terminal of the letter a of Akzidenz Grotesk 'halbfett'). In addition, each letter of the alphabet has a unique individual design, and the alphabet has also a unique letter spacing system.

It is worth noting that Akzidenz Grotesk[11] and similar sans serif typefaces had been revived by type manufacturers in continental Europe during the 1950s and that Berthold had started to re-issue the Akzidenz family in 1955.[12] Akzidenz Grotesk had quickly reached canonical status within the idiom of the high modernist 'Swiss typography' of the late 1950s, and had also reached the English speaking world. Furthermore, Linotype issued the Berthold Akzidenz Grotesk series 57 (normal) and 58 'halbfett' for linecasting machines in 1959. This was before the more regularised and enclosed sans serif typefaces like Folio, Univers, Neue Haas Grotesk/Helvetica, Mercator and Recta – all with horizontally cut terminals – became the dominant idiom.

Like the DIN alphabet suggested by the Anderson committee, Kinneir's new design is characterised by obliquely cut terminals as well as relatively open semi-enclosed counters of letters like a, c, e and s (figure 1).[13] However, the DIN alphabet suffers from rather narrow and rectangular letterforms, and the terminals of its capitals with semi-enclosed counters are cut at inconsistent angles.

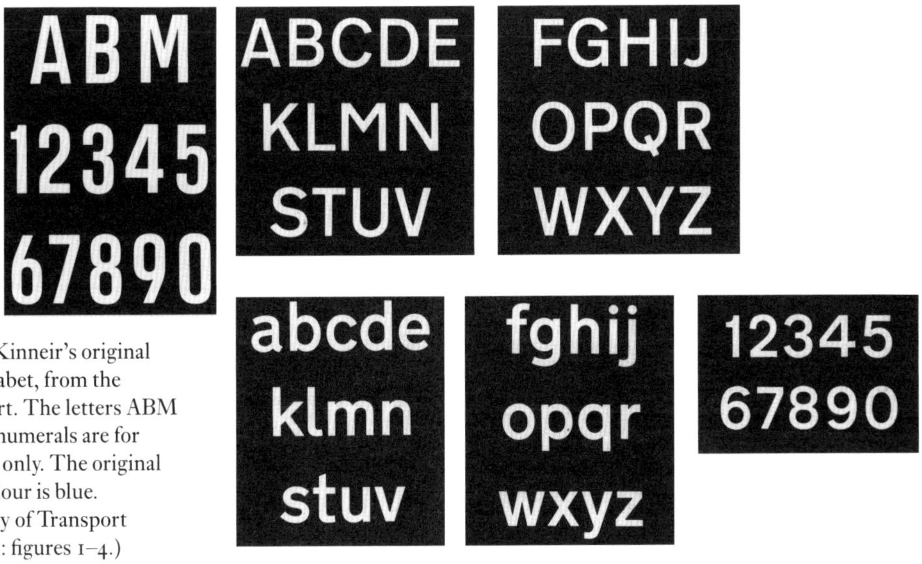

Figure 1. Jock Kinneir's original motorway alphabet, from the Anderson report. The letters ABM and associated numerals are for route-numbers only. The original background colour is blue.
(From: Ministry of Transport 1962, pp. 36–41: figures 1–4.)

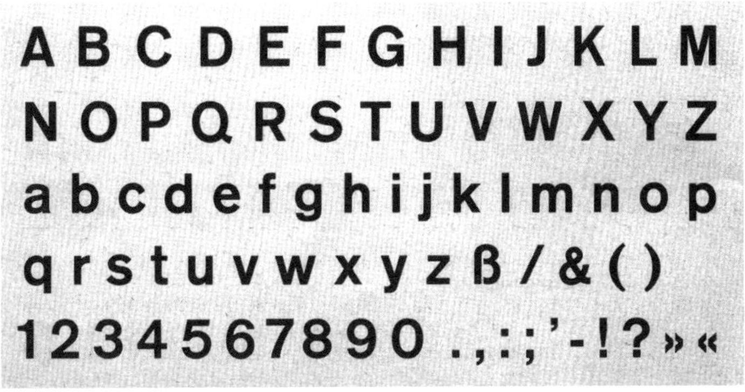

Figure 2. Akzidenz Grotesk 'halbfett' in a Berthold specimen from *c.* 1960 (*Die «klassische» Grotesk*, Probe nr. 462).

Kinneir's new design got the committee's full support, as well as 'almost unanimous' support from the consultative organisations.[14] When designing the sans serif alphabet, Kinneir and Calvert performed informal 'low-tech' experiments: with reflective material in an underground garage in order to determine a sensible weight; and in Hyde Park in London in order to determine sensible appearance-widths and a sensible x-height. In addition, informal experiments were performed in order to create an appropriate letter spacing system. Kinneir later commented on other aspects of the creation of the sans serif letterforms in question:

> The basis of the letter design was the need for forms not to clog when viewed in headlights at a distance. For this reason counters … had to be kept open and gaps prevented from closing. Also, as pointillist painting has shown, forms tend to merge when viewed from a distance, and this suggested a wider letter spacing than is usual in continuous text. (Kinneir 1984, p. 344)

The public controversy

14. Ministry of Transport 1962, p. 4. Specimens of the alphabet appeared, without a name, in the Andersen committee's report (i.e. Ministry of Transport 1962, pp. 35–39).

It was exactly this letterform that – after appearing on the first experimental motorway signs put up in 1959 – generated the most heat and provoked a public controversy on letterform legibility. The controversy was present in the columns of publications as diverse as *New*

15. The following chronological list is not exhaustive. Letter to the editor of *The Times*, 17 March 1959, p. 11, by Brooke Crutchley, printer to the University of Cambridge; attacking Kinneir's work. Letter to the editor of *The Times* 20 March 1959, p. 13, by Noel Carrington, an editor, designer and member of the advisory committee; supporting Kinneir. Letter to the editor of *The Times* 24 March 1959, p. 13, by J[ohn]. G. Dreyfus, and by G. S. Bagley, both attacking Kinneir's work. Editorial note under the heading 'Better traffic signs' in *New Scientist*: vol. 5, no. 124, 2 April 1959, p. 731. Main editorial article, 'Which signs for motorways?', in *Design* no. 129, Sept. 1959, pp. 28–32 (*Design* 1959). This article reported a discussion meeting organised by the journal (initiated by Brooke Crutchley, according to Crutchley 1980, p. 133), with contributors such as: a car manufacturer, a traffic sign manufacturer, the Ministry of Transport, the Road Research Laboratory, a landscape architect, Dr E. C. Poulton from the Medical Research Council's Applied Psychology Research Unit in Cambridge, David Kindersley, Jock Kinneir, Brooke Crutchley, as well as other designers and typographers. Letters to the editor of *Design*, no. 132, Dec. 1959, p. 71 (by Herbert Spencer, and by Aidron Duckworth). Letters to the editor of *Design*, no. 133, Jan. 1960, pp. 75, 77 (by Ernest Hoch, and by Norbert Dutton). An article by David Kindersley in *Traffic Engineering & Control*, Dec. 1960, pp. 463–5 (Kindersley 1960). A note in the 'Peterborough column' in the *Daily Telegraph*, 8 March 1961, and a follow up note a week or so later. Kindersley also appeared in *Cambridge Daily News*, 9 March 1961. Subsequently, in August 1961, the two papers by Christie and Rutley at the Road Research Laboratory, were published in respectively *Roads and Road Construction* (1961b) and *Design* (1961c). Comments were invited from the designers Herbert Spencer, Reynolds Stone and Colin Forbes; these were appended to the article in *Design*. Letters to the editor of *Design* followed up the debate in subsequent issues: In no. 154, October 1961, pp. 87, 89, by Hans Schmoller, and by David Kindersley. In no. 155, November 1961, p. 77, by Colin Forbes. In no. 156, December 1961, pp. 81, 83, by A.G. Long.

16. Letter from Jock Kinneir to Ministry of Transport, dated 17 March 1961. Letter from Ministry of Transport to Kinneir, dated 24 March 1961. (RTC.51/2/03. Margaret Calvert, London.)

17. Christie and Rutley 1961b, p. 239. See also (PRO: MT 126/1, Advisory Committee on Traffic Signs for Motorways: Interim Report, p. 3).

18. Kindersley had been in dialogue with the Ministry of Transport since 1949 when he had proposed for the Ministry that his new street name-plate alphabet (of seriffed

Scientist, Design, Roads and Road Construction, Traffic Engineering and Control, The Times, The Daily Telegraph, The Observer and *Cambridge Daily News*.[15] In March 1961 BBC Television planned a debate between Kinneir and his opponent David Kindersley in the 'Tonight' programme. However, the Ministry of Transport advised Kinneir not to participate, while reassuring Kinneir that he had the committee's full support.[16]

In particular, the radical solution of employing small letters with initial capitals – never before used on standard British road signs[17] – instead of using capitals only, was heatedly debated. Nevertheless, the use of sans serif instead of seriffed letters was also debated in this unique instance of a public discussion of letterform legibility.

The disgruntled opposition to Kinneir's solution was led by the 'traditionalist' letter cutter and lettering artist David Kindersley,[18] a former apprentice and assistant of Eric Gill, and Brooke Crutchley, the printer to Cambridge University, both linked with the British mid-century typographic establishment (in which Stanley Morison was a central figure). I can only guess that this 'establishment', as well as being suspicious of continental modernism, must have been seriously offended by the fact that a major national letterform project had been initiated and partly implemented without it having been consulted.[19] During the debate David Kindersley alleged that Kinneir lacked the basic competence and skill expected of a professional designer. He asserted that the reason why motorists could read Kinneir's direction signs 'is purely the result of their size and not due to any particular skill in their design', and further that size 'is only one of the many points a designer must bear in mind, and [it] is the easiest to determine'. He described Kinneir's alphabet as 'ill-chosen' and the road number figures as not conforming 'with the simplest rules of legibility'. He also described the layout of the direction signs as 'exceedingly inferior' (Kindersley 1960).

It was an illustrated article in *The Times* on 2 December 1958,[20] showing Kinneir's direction signs which were to be tested under actual traffic conditions at the soon-to-open Preston by-pass, that first provoked Kindersley (who had served the Ministry on several occasions in the past).[21] The article in *The Times* led to an instant reaction. The very

capitals) should be adapted as the single standard in Britain. Although Ministry engineers supported the proposal, the Royal Fine Art Commission rejected his proposal (PRO: MT 95/28 1947–1952; MT 95/29 1952–1963; MT 1166; MT 126/1 1955–1968). The alphabet was approved by the Ministry of Transport in 1952 as one of several for street names (Ministry of Transport Circular no. 671, 28th May 1952), and Kindersley was engaged to advise on the spacing of all the recommended alphabets (the circular did not preclude the *ad hoc* use of other alphabets). Kindersley's alphabet was later to be widely used for street nameplates throughout Britain. James Mosley (1964, p. 48) has positively described it as 'using the Trajan idiom with vigour', while Alan Bartram (1978, fig. 59) has referred to it as a 'sluggish letterform' with 'malformed stumps of serifs'. However, at least two versions of this letter-

form seem to be in existence. The name-plate depicted in Mosley 1964 (and in Harrison 2000, p. 29) is a rather heavy-weight, vigorous, *and* beautiful interpretation of the Trajan idiom, while those shown in Dreyfus 1957 (p. 38) and in Baines 1999/2000 (p. 11), are rather anaemic and quaint looking.

19. See also Brooke Crutchley in his autobiography *To be a printer* (1984, pp. 128–140).

20. Kinneir was interviewed on BBC Radio in the 'Today' programme on 5 December 1958. (Margaret Calvert, London)

21. The article was based on a Ministry press notice on 'Motorway traffic signs: experiments on Preston by-pass motorway', which were to be tested for a while under actual traffic conditions, and an attached 'press summary' of an interim report of the 'Advisory committee on traffic signs for motorways'; dated 1 December 1958. This

was less than two weeks before the Prime Minister Harold Macmillan opened this first motorway stretch in Britain. Practical demonstrations of various combinations of messages, letterforms and background colour had been carried out in daylight and darkness for members of the Anderson committee at Hendon Airfield on 18 August, while 'driving at speed' along the runways with committee member Lord Waleran (a former racing driver!) behind the steering wheel. (PRO: MT 126/1). Work on the 8-mile Preston by-pass had begun in 1956; it later became part of the M6 motorway (Charlesworth 1984, p. 1, 35ff).

22. PRO: MT 126/1.
23. PRO: MT 126/1.
24. Brooke Crutchley in *The Times*, March 17, 1959, p. 11.
25. Most notably David Kindersley, Brooke Crutchley, John Dreyfus and G. S. Bagley (see note 15).
26. See especially Kindersley 1960.

Figure 3. *left*: a pre-Kinneir, pre-motorway, directional road sign. (Christie and Rutley 1961b, p. 239: fig. 1). *right*: a Kinneir directional motorway sign. (From Ministry of Transport 1962, p. 59: fig. 38)

Figure 4 (*below*). An illustration from Kindersley 1960, showing a sign suggested by himself (left) and a Kinneir sign (right). Kindersley's caption reads: 'Examples of signs to illustrate the better legibility [of] upper-case alphabet (left) to lower-case (right)'. In his text, Kindersley comments on Kinneir's sign: 'Apart from the ill-chosen type, the height of the sign is still further exaggerated by large areas of wasted space, resulting from the off-centre and asymmetrical contemporary typographical fashion.' (Kindersley 1960, p. 464)

same day Kindersley wrote to an old contact in the Ministry of Transport, a Mr Hadfield, asking for more information and a meeting. He stated that the letters on the direction signs 'don't appear to be very legible' and suggested that if lower case had to be used it should at least be a 'decent lower-case'. In a telephone conversation with Hadfield the following day, after extending his criticism by, among other things, pointing out 'the awful M', Kindersley announced that he would discuss the matter with Mr Brooke Crutchley, the Printer to Cambridge University, 'before deciding whether to make any public criticism'.[22] In further correspondence between Kindersley and Hadfield at the Department during the winter, Kindersley disclosed his work on an alternative 'Mot-serif alphabet', and about the preparation of a letter to the editor of *The Times* by Brooke Crutchley.[23] The letter was published on 17 March 1959; it was this letter that started the public debate under discussion here. Crutchley asserted that Kinneir's solution ignored specialised 'knowledge accumulated over the years' and that there had been some 'misguided work behind the present proposal'.[24]

The 'traditionalists'[25] argued that letterforms for destination names on sign panels are more legible in capitals than in small letters,[26] in spite of the fact that – as their argument goes – words in small letters are more legible for continuous text in books. (It was thus argued that words in small letters make both irregular word shapes *and* familiar word patterns for continuous text, and that this aids recognition.) The reason for preferring all-capitals for sign panels, according to the same argument, was that horizontal eye movements is not an issue on sign panels, and that place names are not familiar word patterns.

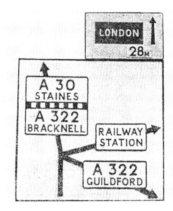

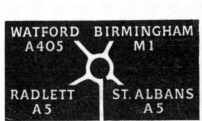
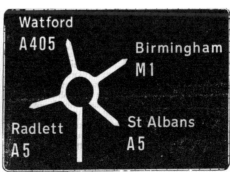

Examples of signs to illustrate the better legibility upper-case alphabet (left) to lower-case (right)

It was also argued that capitals are intrinsically clearer than small letters, especially when compared in the same nominal size. Therefore, the argument went, all-capital signs would allow for considerably smaller sign panels and therefore give large benefits with regard to the cost of production, as well as creating less impact on the landscape, and furthermore, smaller sign panels were easier to be caught in dipped headlights. The reasoning here was that as long as the dominant dimension of capitals (capital height) is bigger than the dominant dimension of small letters (x-height), big conspicuous all-capital lettering could be applied in a given area without the need to allocate space for ascenders and descenders.

It was further argued that serifs would strengthen terminals and thus define letters more clearly from a distance. In fact, David Kindersley proposed a theory of how serifs improve the legibility of letterforms in certain situations:

> Try reading a page of sans-serif lower-case, and then a page of 'normal-face' and you will see at once that the normal one is more readable. The reason for the existence of the serif is clear, and is not just a meaningless tradition. In very small type, or in larger letters to be read at a great distance – in fact, wherever there is a question of distance in relation to size – there is always a loss of definition. The serif reinforces the individual character of the letter exactly where this loss is greatest. (Kindersley 1960, p. 465)[27]

In the same article Kindersley continued his attacks on the motorway alphabet. On the numerals for use in route numbers only (and the associated letters A, B, and M) he commented categorically:

> The road numbers, together with their letters, are even worse than the main alphabet, and do not conform with the simplest rules of legibility or differentiation. (Kindersley 1960, p. 465)

Against the arguments of the traditionalists, it was argued by the supporters of Jock Kinneir[28] that words with initial capitals and small letters provided more differentiated as well as more familiar word-shapes, as opposed to the rectangular and monotonous shapes of all-capital words. Words would therefore be easier to recognise from a distance. It was also claimed that the serifs and the modulated strokes of seriffed (roman) typefaces are not very well suited for reflective material.

The experiments

Comparative experimental research was recommended by several of the participants in the debate, especially at a discussion meeting organized by *Design* magazine.[29] The experiments subsequently undertaken by Christie and Rutley for the Road Research Laboratory[30] were, apparently, conducted as an answer to this demand. To put these experiments in perspective it should be taken into account that Kindersley's challenge was to a process that was already under way. It was not as if the job had been conceived as a public competition or competitive tender. The Anderson committee was fully in favour of Kinneir's proposal – based on parameters set by the committee itself. I think it is correct to say that the committee had no plans whatsoever

27. Reiterated in Kindersley 1974.

28. Most notably Noel Carrington, Herbert Spencer and Aidron Duckworth (see note 15). As a designer to a government committee, Kinneir did not (and could not) publicly reply to the attacks on his work.

29. The article 'Which signs for motorways?' reported the discussion meeting (*Design* 1959, pp. 28–32). See note 15 for the participants. Both sides claimed support from existing experimental legibility research (mainly on the question of capitals versus small letters, but also on the question of serif versus sans serif). See also a letter to the editor from Noel Carrington in *The Times*, 20 March 1959, p. 13; a letter to the editor from John Dreyfus in *The Times*, 24 March 1959, p. 13; as well as Kindersley 1960, p. 464. Also see references to existing research – for example to Forbes *et al.* (1950 [sic]) – in Christie and Rutley (1961a, 1961b, 1961c), in Moore and Christie (1960, 1963), and in the Anderson report (Ministry of Transport 1962, p. 4). Other references to existing research can be found in Reynolds Stone's invited comment (p. 61) appended to Christie and Rutley's paper in *Design* (Stone 1961); and in a letter to the editor from David Kindersley, in *Design*, no. 154, 1961, pp. 87, 89.

30. 'To assist the [Anderson] committee a substantial research programme was carried out in the Road User Section on the effects of factors such as lettering, size of sign, colour and lighting on the visibility and legibility of signs' (Charlesworth 1987, p. 120).

to abandon Kinneir's solution, regardless of the outcome of the Road Research Laboratory's experiment. The Kindersley 'challenge' was regarded with irritation in the Anderson committee as well as in the Ministry of Transport. As was pointed out in a letter to Jock Kinneir from the ministry:

> You are already in a strong position vis-a-vis your detractors; it is you who were commissioned by the Department to do the job, it is your signs that have been erected on the motorways, and you can be sure of the solid support of the Committee for what you have done.[31]

In fact, Kinneir and the committee members tacitly regarded Kindersley as an indefatigable and annoying detractor who carried out a campaign based on 'tendentious claims and half-truths' against both the committee's and Kinneir's work.[32]

Kindersley had stated optimistically that: 'No decision should be finally and publicly announced on the M1 signs until the facts are established by the Road Research Laboratory' (Kindersley 1960, p. 465). Dr E. C. Poulton[33] from the Applied Psychology Unit of the Medical Research Council, who participated in the discussion meeting organised by *Design*, 'was in no doubt that the facts could be established – providing the criteria could be agreed in the first place' (*Design* 1959, no. 129, p. 30).

Four different types of letterform were employed in the experiments:

- sans serif letters of capitals only, based on designs by Edward Johnston, commissioned by the Road Research Laboratory from the chief critic of Kinneir's solution, letter cutter David Kindersley;
- seriffed letters of capitals only, commissioned by the Road Research Laboratory from David Kindersley;
- Jock Kinneir's sans serif small letters (with initial capitals); by then already employed on the Preston by-pass in Lancashire;
- the same letters by Kinneir as above, but in a smaller size and applied with more interlinear space and more generous margins.

The aim of the experiment was to find out which of these types of letterform could be read at the greatest distance in order 'to keep the angle between the driver's line of sight and the road ahead as small as possible' (Christie and Rutley 1961c, p. 59). However, the experiment also aimed at investigating the question of capitals versus small letters, and in addition, investigating 'the value of serifs ... because it has been suggested ... that serifed lettering is more legible than sans-serif lettering' (1961b, p. 240). Christie and Rutley alleged that the question of sans serif versus seriffed letterforms was only examined with respect to the two capital letter styles employed (since no small letters with serifs were included in this multi-variable experiment).

Altogether 6336 reading distances were recorded.[34] The experiments were conducted in an airfield at Benson in South Oxfordshire. In order to speed up the experiments the signs were attached to a car moving towards stationary observers instead of the opposite natural way (see figure 6). Christie and Rutley sensibly pointed out that this reversing should not affect the relative order between the letterforms.[35] The size of the letters on the test signs were around five times smaller

31. Letter from the Ministry of Transport to Jock Kinneir, 24 March, 1961, Ref. RTC.51/2/03. (This is the letter where the ministry advised Kinneir not to participate in a television debate with Kindersley.) (Margaret Calvert, London.)

32. Letter from Jock Kinneir to the Ministry of Transport, 17 March 1961; letter from the committee chairman Colin Anderson to Fred Salfield of the *Daily Telegraph*, 8 March 1961, complaining about the misinformed pro-Kindersley coverage in the newspaper's 'Peterborough' column the very same day, where it was reported that the Anderson committee was about to report to the Minister of Transport in Kindersley's favour; letter from Colin Anderson to Jock Kinneir, 6 April 1961. (Margaret Calvert, London.)

33. Poulton published several research papers on legibility in the late 1950s and the early 1960s, in journals like *American Journal of Psychology, Ergonomics* and *Journal of Applied Psychology*.

34. Christie and Rutley 1961a, p. 6.

35. Although Cohen (1981), according to Hughes and Cole (1986), demonstrated that eye movement behaviour is different in a laboratory situation from when actually driving on the road, Hughes and Cole claim that the pattern of eye movements is not a critical factor in the conspicuity of objects (Hughes & Cole 1986, pp. 1108–09).

than for Kinneir's real signs already in use on the Preston by-pass. However, absolute size and absolute distances were not in question here, and had been dealt with experimentally earlier (see *Design*, no. 129, 1959). Sizes were probably anyway expected to vary for different applications and situations.

The mean reading distances – where the longer the better – were, in descending order:

- 247 ft for David Kindersley's seriffed capitals;
- 240 ft for Jock Kinneir's sans serif small letters with initial capitals;
- 239 ft for the Edward Johnston-based sans serif capitals;
- 212 ft for Jock Kinneir's letterforms in a smaller size and with generous margins.

Figure 5. One of the 24 basic signs that were used in the experiment (here shown in four alphabets). The total number of signs was 96, based on four alphabets and 24 basic signs (6 single-name destination signs, 6 two-name destination signs, 6 three-name destination signs, and 6 message signs like 'Stop' and 'No entry'). From the top: Kindersley's 'Edward Johnston' alphabet; Kindersley's own seriffed alphabet; Kinneir's sans serif alphabet; and Kinneir's sans serif alphabet in smaller size and with generous margins. (Christie and Rutley 1961b, p. 240: figure 3c)

Figure 6. 'The experiment was greatly speeded up by mounting the signs on a vehicle and driving them towards a group of 10–15 stationary observers seated on a tiered platform.' Note the 'margins' of the board on which the signs are mounted. The subjects in the experiments were Royal Air Force volunteers, at Benson airfield, Oxfordshire. (Christie and Rutley 1961a, figure 4. The photograph was published in Christie and Rutley 1961b, p. 242, as figure 4; and later published in Mijksenaar 1971, p. 30.).

Discussion

While discussing their results, Christie and Rutley asserted that the difference in favour of Kindersley's seriffed capitals over the two sans serif letter styles was statistically significant – 'about 3 per cent … i.e. the difference is unlikely to be due to chance' (1961c, p. 60). However they added that spacing, layout, and width to height ratio of the letters, might have been confounding factors. Nevertheless, they seem to have overlooked that – according to figures given in the text – the height of Kindersley's seriffed capital letters was at least 25 per cent larger than the dominant dimension of the largest version of Kinneir's sans serif letters, their x-height. Thus, since reading distance is to a large extent a function of letter size, results more favourable to Kinneir's letterforms could have been produced by increasing that size.

However, the Road Research Laboratory (as opposed to the Anderson committee), seemed persuaded by Kindersley and his supporters' heavily promoted view that the competing letterforms should be compared while positioned tightly into areas of equal size hardly without surrounding space, and by referring to the production cost per square unit of a sign. Under this unrealistic condition, capitals will inevitably create a more prominent visual image than small letters. This is because small letters will have to accommodate extra interlinear spacing for ascenders and descenders. Their visual size, expressed by x-height, will under this condition have to be smaller. Not only does this 'tightly crammed on an equal area' argument rely on an unrealistic condition (both printed matter and sign panels usually rely on relatively large areas of space around the text), it also disregards a basic heuristic rule among designers: that interlinear spacing needs to be larger for text in capitals than for text in small letters. Furthermore, it also disregards the fact that capitals are wider than small letters and so need considerably more space width-wise, something which might become a critical factor on sign panels with long destination names. Some long destination names even needed to be abbreviated or contracted on some sign-panels, and restricted space in some circumstances demanded economy in sign width.[36] Nevertheless, the Anderson report concluded this debate in the following way:

> We feel … that in designing a traffic sign regard must be paid to the space around the lettering as well as to the lettering itself, and that a sign that completely filled the space available would be so un-attractive as to be quite unacceptable. (Ministry of Transport 1962, p. 4)

Kinneir pointed out that 'The criterion requiring an economic use of sign surface was to be largely overridden by the need to achieve clarity of layout on the more complex signs' (Kinneir 1971, p. 10). A similar point of view had also been present in the internal discussions of the committee, where it was asserted that instead of filling the space available, a relatively large area of uninterrupted blue background against the landscape background was desirable in order to reduce background noise and improve the 'target value' of the sign.[37] Note that the experimental signs employed by the Road Research Laboratory, probably for similar reasons ('target value'), were mounted on a large khaki-painted panel, providing a wide margin, on top of the car that moved towards the stationary observers (see figure 6).

36. The Anderson committee was fully aware of this in its discussions (PRO: MT126/1: 'Minutes of the twenty-second meeting' [of the Anderson committee] 25 April 1960). See also the discussion in the Anderson report (Ministry of Transport 1962, p. 9). Also of relevance here is a discussion in the Worboys report on situations 'when site conditions restrict the width of signs' (Ministry of Transport 1963, p. 10). See also PRO: MT 116/6: Appendix A to Committee Paper no. 4 (a talk on traffic signs by R. L. Moore).

37. Committee 'Notes', 29 February 1960; and committee 'Minutes' of the 22nd meeting, 25 April 1960; as well as a letter from Jock Kinneir to the Ministry of Transport, 17 March 1961. (Margaret Calvert, London.)

38. For a brief but useful discussion on the technical concept of 'statistical significance' see Pedhazur and Schmelkin 1991, pp. 202–3.

39. At an earlier instance Spencer had referred disapprovingly to Kindersley's alphabet as 'quaintly rustic letter forms' (Letter to the editor of *Design*, no. 132, December 1959, p. 71).

40. Letter from Jock Kinneir to the Ministry of Transport, 17 March 1961. (Margaret Calvert, London.)

41. Cyril Burt's and (fictitious?) co-author's once acclaimed article 'A psychological study of typography' was published in 1955 in the journal which Burt edited, *The British Journal of Statistical Psychology*. Burt's almost identical monograph, bearing the same title, with a foreword by Stanley Morison, was published by Cambridge University Press in 1959. The positive reception of these two publications until the early 1980s, among both researchers and designers, has been thoroughly dealt with by Rooum (1981) and Hartley and Rooum (1983). They have convincingly shown that Burt's dubious if not fraudulent practices also extended into his work on legibility and typography (see e.g. Hearnshaw 1979). Note that Robert B. Joynson's attempt to rehabilitate Burt (Joynson 1989) ignores Rooum and Hartley's devastating articles, and that Rooum and Hartley's articles are not mentioned in Mackintosh's collection (1995).

ABCDEFG HIJKLMN OPQRSTU VWXYZ

Figure 7. Davis Kindersley's capitals-only seriffed alphabet. (*Design* 1959, p. 30)

Christie and Rutley seemed to be fully aware that the technical concept of 'statistical significance' does not express meaningful significance or substantial meaningfulness.[38] They concluded that 'the most remarkable feature of the results for the three … scripts is that the reading distances are so nearly equal … the difference is so small that caution is necessary in interpreting its meaning' (Christie and Rutley 1961b, p. 243), and 'the results do clearly indicate … that none of the three scripts tested has any appreciable advantage over the others with regard to legibility' (Christie and Rutley 1961c, p. 60). It is thus reasonable to claim that no significant difference in legibility was found. In their conclusion Christie and Rutley also noted that the small difference between the two capital letter styles (one seriffed and one sans serif) was not necessarily based on the serifs or lack thereof, but might depend on other variables.

Christie and Rutley finally concluded: 'Since there is little difference in legibility between the different types of lettering, it seems reasonable to make the choice on aesthetic grounds' (1961c, p. 60). They went even further and suggested that 'there are grounds for believing that aesthetic questions may be at the root of the controversy' (1961b, p. 243). In the final Anderson report, it is admitted that 'taste plays so important a part, as we believe it should' (Ministry of Transport 1962, p. 5). Herbert Spencer in his comment in *Design*, stressed that aesthetic consideration – 'taste, tradition, relevance and fashion' – were of utmost importance. He clearly expressed his disapproval of Kindersley's 'partially' seriffed letters, which he described as 'clumsy' and as ignoring 'both taste and tradition' (Spencer 1961).[39] Also Reynolds Stone seemed unhappy about Kindersley's 'unusually seriffed capitals' and he complimented Kinneir's sans serif letters. Nevertheless, he suggested that if 'good' small seriffed letters had been included in the tests, they might have outdone the others (Stone 1961).

Kinneir referred, although not in public, to Kindersley's proposed alphabet as having 'mis-serifs': 'As far as appearance goes I cannot imagine even the most obdurant philistine wanting to cover England with 'mis-serifs!'[40] And in a much later account, Kinneir referred to the committee's view of Kindersley's alphabet as 'grotesquely ugly' (Kinneir 1983, p. 20).

Unsurprisingly, Cyril Burt's name was called upon in the debate:

> Fashionable or not, the use of sans meant ignoring experts like the psychologist Sir Cyril Burt, who 'has recently recalled and reaffirmed scientific findings that "for word recognition a sans serif type face was the worst of all" '. (Stone 1961, here quoting P. M. Handover's recently published 'Letters without serifs', which again quotes Burt.)[41]

David Kindersley defended his design. In a letter to the editor of *Design* in a later issue, he applauded the tests undertaken by the Road Research Laboratory. He however urged that 'the conclusions drawn from it are bad – really bad' (letter to the editor, *Design*, no. 154, 1961, pp. 87, 89). He pointed out that the tests were not performed at 'real distances'. He claimed, referring to a study by the prolific American researchers Paterson and Tinker (1946) on the legibility of newspaper headlines, that both capital legibility and seriffed letter legibility decrease at a lesser rate (assumingly with an increase in distance) than for both small letters and for sans serif letters. Furthermore, he claimed that his letters for motorway signs 'can be read from at least 175 ft further away than the existing lower case signs [i.e. Kinneir's] with equal areas' (p. 89). I can only guess that this figure is based on calculations where several quantities are included – for example the differences of the results between his and Kinneir's alphabets, the difference between the test distance and a larger distance, and 'the decrease at a lesser rate' thesis referred to above.

Kinneir's supporter Herbert Spencer brought up a fundamental reservation about the value of experimental research, and cautioned:

> Such tests of lettering as these are therefore useful in disposing of pseudo-scientific arguments, but in cases where the results strongly favour a particular design they must, to be of any practical use to designers, be elaborated upon so that we can clearly understand why one design functions more effectively than another.
> (Spencer 1961).

It is interesting to observe in retrospect that the public debate on these new direction signs focused on only one – and a rather low-level – aspect of the new direction signs, their letter design. One of the letters to the editor of *Design* in the aftermath of the presentation of Christie and Rutley's research came from A. G. Long (assumingly not a designer, perhaps a road engineer). He applied what today might be called a usability perspective and accused the research of suffering 'from an unnecessarily restricted consideration of some aspects and an unduly indiscriminate study of others'. He pointed out that the question of colour seemed to have been ignored, and the same applied to performance in bad weather, or in the dark while illuminated by different kinds of artificial lighting along the road and from the car. 'All these are surely more urgent problems of road design than a finicking survey of the effect of serifs on capital letters on large boards displayed in good conditions on the best roads.' (letter to the editor, *Design*, no. 156, 1961, pp. 81, 83). Note however that the discussions in the committee and the advice from the consultative organisations predominantly focused on more high level questions, like: the content of, and logical relationships between, the many categories of direction signs, as well as colour and illumination, and mounting and siting.

From the Anderson committee to the Worboys committee

Jock Kinneir was subsequently engaged as designer to the Ministry of Transport's Worboys committee (1961–1963) on traffic signs for 'all-purpose' roads. The Worboys committee was served by a Working Party, with officers from the Ministry of Transport and the Road Research Laboratory. Kinneir was not a member of either the committee or the working party, but he attended practically all their meetings, at which he frequently demonstrated new design proposals.[42]

Kindersley's challenge was however not laid to rest. The 'merits of upper and lower case lettering' was constantly recurring at meetings in the Worboys committee, and considerable resources were employed to deal with the question. The admission was that 'it was essential that

42. PRO: MT 116/1–17.

[the committee] recommendations should be on a firm basis'[43] and that Kindersley should 'be given a full and fair hearing'.[44]

At the second committee meeting Christie from the Road Research Laboratory introduced the subject by describing the comparative research from 1961 on Kindersley's and Kinneir's letterforms. He concluded that there were 'remarkably little differences'.[45] In a later meeting the committee summed up Christie's presentation: 'that from the point of view of functional effectiveness there was little to choose between upper and lower case lettering; on grounds of taste and appearance they were firmly in favour of lower case'.[46] According to a tabulated review of comments from the 26 organisations consulted by the Worboys committee, none requested upper case letterforms, and only two explicitly requested lower case.[47]

Two 'Committee documents' were dedicated to the question of 'upper case' versus 'lower case': 'A comparison of two designs for a stack-type advanced direction sign'[48] (figure 8), and 'The claims of Mr. Kindersley on behalf of upper case lettering on road signs'.[49] In the latter it was revealed that

> David Kindersley during April continued the campaign already conducted with Sir Colin Anderson's Committee on Motorway Signs to urge the superiority of upper-case for road signs. His argument is that upper-case letters, because they do not waste space with ascenders and descenders, can be larger and therefore more legible in a given space than lower case letters. This was specially true of serifed upper-case. Therefore, if upper-case lettering were used, road signs could be considerably smaller and less expensive.

An experiment and a comparison test between signs with Kindersley's letterforms and signs with Kinneir's letterforms were performed by the Road Research Laboratory for the Worboys committee.[50] The experiment and the comparison test are both described in 'The claims of Mr. Kindersley … '.[51]

The experiment involved 13 subjects who were passengers in a car. Interestingly, while implicitly discussing internal validity problems in this multi-variate experiment (posed by confounding factors such as variations in background colour etc.), the Road Research Laboratory nevertheless concluded that

> the mean legibility distance for the place-names on Mr Kindersley's [upper case] sign was 3.4 per cent greater than that for the RRL sign [with Kinneir's lower case]. The difference, however, was not statistically significant, i.e. it could have been due to chance.[52]

On this background, the Committee asserted that

> the results of this analysis was broadly in agreement with previous experiments of the RRL in 1961 … However, it was considered that a fuller comparison was necessary before the claims of Mr. Kindersley could be dismissed.[53]

A kind of preference study ('comparison tests') was therefore also conducted by the Road Research Laboratory, involving groups of 'observers not on the RRL staff to place the signs in order of merit'. The two Kindersley signs included in these 'comparison tests' (with two different background colours) came out respectively seventh and

43. PRO: MT 116/5. Committee minutes 5, 31 May 1962.
44. PRO: MT 116/1. Working Party minutes 14, 7 June 1962.
45. PRO: MT 116/5. Committee minutes 2, 22 February 1962.
46. PRO: MT 116/5. Committee minutes 4, 26 April 1962.
47. PRO: MT 116/6. Committee paper no. 4, 'Direction signs', 9 April 1962.
48. PRO: MT 116/8. Committee document no. 11, May 1962.
49. PRO: MT 116/8. Committee document no. 14, 10 September 1962.
50. PRO: MT 116/8. Committee document no. 11, May 1962.
51. PRO: MT 116/8. Committee document no. 14, 10 September 1962.
52. PRO: MT 116/8. Committee document no. 11, May 1962.
53. PRO: MT 116/8. Committee document no. 14, 10 September 1962.

54. PRO: MT 116/8. Committee document no. 14, 10 September 1962.

55. PRO: MT 116/8. Committee document no. 14, 10 September 1962.

56. PRO: MT 126/1. 'Note of a meeting', 8 August 1963 (this note prescribes several changes of features used on early motorway signs and shown in the Anderson Report). MT 126/1. 'Loose minute' of a meeting on 'Motorway signs', 8 December 1964.

eleventh 'in efficiency' out of 13 signs. Two signs designed by Kinneir and two signs designed by the RRL (all four in lower case letters) came out first.[54]

After receiving the RRL's results for this experiment and for the comparison test, the Worboys committee closed the matter and finally concluded that 'the members of the committee agreed that a full and fair hearing had been given to Mr. Kindersley's claims'.[55]

From the motorway alphabet to 'Transport medium' and 'Transport heavy'

For the Worboys committee and thus for Britain's 'all-purpose roads' Kinneir developed two slightly modified variants of his motorway alphabet (with, for example, a shortened hook on the lower case j). The two alphabets were named Transport Medium and Transport Heavy. The 'medium' was for white letters on a blue or green (dark) background (see figure 11), and the 'heavy' was for black letters on a white or yellow (light) background (see Ministry of Transport 1963, pp. 97–102) (see figure 12). However, an alternative style for route-numbering was not included for 'all-purpose roads', as for the motorways (see note 13). The elegantly sloping lines of the arrows that symbolised the roads ahead on the motorway advance direction signs became straightened out on the Worboys signs for all-purpose roads (compare figure 3 with figure 9). Furthermore, for Worboys the model of direction sign layout inherited from the Anderson committee was also 'redesigned', leading to much smaller sign areas.

Soon after the publication of the Worboys Report in April 1963 (before the subsequent regulations went through Parliament and came into operation in January 1965), meetings were held in the Ministry in order 'to discuss the impact of the Worboys Report on motorway signs'.[56] It was decided to harmonise as far as possible the design and layout of the two types of British direction signs – on the lines laid down for all-purpose road signs.

Figure 8. *left*: Map-type advance direction sign for a roundabout junction on an 'all-purpose' primary route. The background colour is green. (From: Ministry of Transport 1963, pp. 34–35, 122).
right: Stack-type advance direction sign. The background colour is green. (From: Ministry of Transport 1963, p. 24)

9b

Figure 9. (a) Top and middle: route confirmatory sign and direction sign. The background colour is green. Bottom: direction sign to motorway for use on all-purpose road. The background colour is blue. (From Ministry of Transport 1963, pp. 120, 127). (b) Advance direction sign before a junction. The background colour is green. (From Ministry of Transport 1963, p. 120).

9a

Figure 10. A flag-type direction sign for local use. (Photograph provided by Margaret Calvert)

  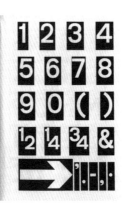

Figure 11. Transport Medium, for use on signs with dark backgrounds. (From Ministry of Transport 1963, pp. 97–99)

Figure 12. Transport Heavy, for use on signs with white backgrounds. (From Ministry of Transport 1963, pp. 100–101)

In retrospect

It was decided to use Kinneir's sans serif alphabets of small letters and initial capitals, as well as his complete sign system, for both motorways and all-purpose roads.[57] Some of the many prominent absences in his motorway directional signs were: no serifs, no boxes around destination name and road number, no barbs on the heads of the arrows that symbolise the road ahead, and, not least, no forced symmetrical or grid-based positioning of destination names.[58] This represented an 'exceedingly inferior layout' and resulted in 'large areas of wasted space' according to Kindersley (1960, p. 464). Although the 'no boxes' feature adhered to an emerging modernist norm in graphic design (meaningful groupings were to be signalled, minimalistically, by spatial relationships alone),[59] it was also based on the wish of the Anderson committee, and was in accordance with the 1949 Geneva protocol.[60] Furthermore, eliminating the boxes around each destination name and road number, while keeping the map-like[61] organisation of the destination signs, allowed for considerably larger lettering on the same sign area.[62]

57. Ministry of Transport, 1962; 1963; and subsequent regulations and reviews, referred to in Department of Transport 1991, p. 12ff.

58. 'We went for the utmost simplicity, cutting out everything which didn't actually say anything (like serifs on letters, and boxes round lettering) and went on cutting and cutting until we were left with the residue, the important residue, and then gave that the greatest value possible.' (Kinneir 1983, p. 19).

59. 'Instead a system of layout was devised in which related items are related spatially and unrelated items are derelated spatially' (Kinneir 1989, p. 4).

60. Letter from Ministry of Transport to Kinneir, signed R. L. Huddy, 12 June 1958. RTC 53/4/024 Pt 4. (Margaret Calvert, London.) See also Froshaug 1963, illustration on p. 46.

61. A layout of the approaching junction and destinations ahead, marked with arrows and with the associated destination names distributed accordingly.

62. Moore and Christie 1960, p. 815.

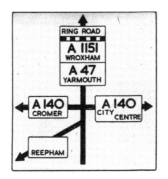 

Figure 13. Prototype signs, probably made at the Road Research Laboratory.
Left: A complex intersection as shown in the 1957 regulations.
Right: The same intersection without boxes enclosing the destination names – which allows for considerable larger letters. (From Moore and Christie 1960, p. 815)

Figure 14. Jock Kinneir overseeing signs under manufacture. (From *Sign World* 1967, p. 676)

Kinneir's rather neutral sans serif letterforms were, compared with Kindersley's somewhat unusual seriffed capitals, undoubtedly more in line with contemporary aesthetic preferences among designers and taste trend-setters. To suggest that the final decision of the Anderson committee was taken already before the Road Research Laboratory performed the tests at Benson airfield in 1960 is perhaps to overstate the issue, but nevertheless, a feeling that the experiments were some kind of play to the gallery – only necessitated by the public debate and performed in order to shrug it off – is hard to avoid. Nevertheless, Kinneir's solution of lower case sans serif letterforms corresponded more with the practice in neighbouring European countries,[63] as well as with direction signs on the American interstate highways[64] – an important imperative.

Kinneir and many other designers at that time strongly believed that sans serif letterforms – in the combination of small letters and initial capitals – were intrinsically more legible for signing systems than seriffed capitals, due to the more distinctive word shapes they created. They also believed that sans serif letterforms were easier to handle, less 'aesthetically sensitive', and generally more 'forgiving' when actually produced; that is, in various modified forms for various applications, especially with the tools available at the time. Furthermore, if small letters were preferred, then sans serif letters were undoubtedly more aesthetically suited than seriffed letters to relatively short ascenders and descenders (i.e. to large x-heights); hence they demanded less inter-linear space and thus were more practical (Mason 1994).

With the recommendations of the Worboys committee for all-purpose roads, words set in all-capital style were largely reserved for certain mandatory and prohibitory traffic signs. This distinction provided the means for a functional differentiation of certain important signs such as 'STOP' and 'GIVE WAY'.[65]

Noel Carrington, a member of the Anderson committee, argued that since seriffed types are characterised by a high contrast between thick and thin strokes, they 'would almost certainly prove unsuitable when the letters have to consist of reflectionized material to catch the headlights'.[66] In reply, it has to be admitted that Kindersley's sturdy seriffed capitals were unusually low in contrast – probably in order to solve exactly the problem suggested by Carrington. However, this characteristic of Kindersley's design, together with its highly idiosyncratic and unusual serifs, rather than its serifs *per se*, might very well have created exactly the uneasiness that people like Herbert Spencer felt towards it.

Interestingly, the leading figure of the British mid-century typographic establishment, Stanley Morison, who seems not to have participated in the public debate, undermined at least part of the argument of his fellow traditionalists, while addressing a continental public. In a 1962 postscript to a German-language edition of his *First principles of typography*, published in Switzerland in 1966,[67] Morison stressed the practical and pragmatic aspects of using sans serif letter-forms for applications like traffic signs.

> Sanserif type is … quicker, easier and therefore cheaper to make. It is in fact the cheapest of all to make. Its forms can be mastered by the

63. That is, in Germany, Belgium and Holland, but not in France. In fact, 'continental practice was evenly divided in the use of upper or lower-case lettering on direction signs' (PRO: MT 116/5. Committee minutes no. 4, 26 April, 1962).

64. *Design*, no. 129, September 1959, p. 31; Design, no. 132, 1959, p. 71; Moore and Christie 1960, p. 816; Ministry of Transport 1962, p. 4.

65. See for example Ministry of Transport 1963, pp. 10, 103; Moore and Christie 1963, p. 116.

66. Letter to the editor from Noel Carrington, in *The Times*, 20 March 1959, p. 13.

67. See Huib van Krimpen's introduction in a recent edition of *First principles of typography* (Morison 1996, p. xiii).

lowest category of draftsmen. Naturally, municipal architects and others to whom lettering is no more and no less than a necessary evil, gave the medium a cordial welcome, and with reason. That is to say with reason of a natural kind: of self-interest, which is the best – because a material and rational – basis for the choice of sanserif. It is not surprising that sanserif is superseding the serifed style in all transport and street designations. Its economy of cost cannot but make sanserif the universal public medium of communication. (reprinted in Morison 1996, p. 39)

The aftermath

Together with his associate Margaret Calvert,[68] Kinneir came to dominate the design of public wayfinding and signing systems, and their associated sans serif letterforms, in Britain in the next few decades – for motorways and all-purpose roads, airports, the railways, the public hospitals, and the armed forces. Their influence was also felt abroad – for road signs, railway signs and airport signs.[69] Kinneir's motorway signing system has 'been called Britain's true corporate identity' (Rainford 1996, p. 13) as well as 'a house style for Britain' (Baines 1999, p. 27).[70]

However, the dispute did not end in the 1960s. Since then it has come to the surface on many occasions. Several contemporary writers are vigorous supporters of David Kindersley's position of the early 1960s. For example Montague Shaw, in his book on David Kindersley, offered this summary:

> It is one of the misfortunes of the creative person that his sensible work is, from time to time, set aside in favour of a vastly inferior article, by ignorant judges who are swayed by fashion and an uneducated taste. … [David Kindersley's letters] were better in every single case. But the sanserif was used. (Shaw 1989, p. 19)

This account was accentuated in a more politicised manner by the designer James Souttar in a talk given at the Monotype Conference in Cambridge, 1992. Citing Shaw, he described Kinneir's road sign work as belonging to nothing less than 'a vision of shabby utopianism.' (Souttar 1992, p. 5). Other factually unreliable accounts have been published; for example:

> A series of tests carried out by the Road Research Laboratory showed that in terms of recognition and legibility at speed, Kindersley's capitalized serif letters *were greatly superior* to the modernist sans serif, upper-and-lower-case letters. But despite this conclusive result the sans serif was chosen. (Eason and Rookledge 1991, p. 98; my italics)

However, Robin Kinross, who appears prominently among the 'pro-Kinneir historians', celebrates Kinneir's work as a great achievement:[71]

> These signs were the first, in any country, in which 'visual' and 'functional' considerations were fused. They marked a new turn in British typography. And in the subtleties of their letterforms and of their rules of configuration, the signs showed a sophistication beyond the grasp of the title page- and inscription-bound traditionalism. (Kinross 1992, p. 167)

68. Margaret Calvert became a partner in Kinneir, Calvert Associates in 1964. She was head of graphic design at the Royal College of Art (1987–1990).

69. For example (either on motorways, airports or railways) in Australia, in Hong Kong, in the Middle East, in Greece, on the Continent, and in Scandinavia. For instance both the Danish and the Norwegian road sign alphabets are adaptations of the Kinneir Transport alphabet. Both alphabets retain the noticeable round dot on the lower case letters i and j. However, the Danish alphabet, introduced in 1978, is a more direct adaptation – albeit excessively letterspaced compared with the Kinneir original (see Bernsen *et al.* 1996, pp. 30ff). The Norwegian 'Trafikkalfabetet', drawn in the mid 1960s (date given by Erik Hagen at Vegdirektoratet, Oslo) is a far rougher adaptation where e.g. the discriminating 'legibility hook' on the lower case letter l has been removed (see Statens Vegvesen 1987, pp. 381ff).

70. Jock Kinneir gave many lectures at conferences around the world, was interviewed on television and radio on several occasions, and wrote several substantial accounts on his signing systems (e.g. Kinneir 1968; 1970; 1971; 1983; 1984). He published one book, *Words and buildings: the art and practice of public lettering* (1980), and was head of graphic design at the Royal College of Art 1964–1969.

71. See Kinross 1984; 1989; 1992, p. 167; 1994b.

72. Not only did the 1949 UN Geneva protocol inform its work, but four members of the Anderson committee had made a personal inspection of motorway signs in Belgium, Holland and Germany (PRO: MT 126/1, Press notice, 1 Dec. 1958). They had also taken colour slides while touring continental roads (Kinneir 1971, p. 3).

Kinross is not only enthusiastic about the end result of the design process but also attaches great importance to the process itself: as an exemplary model for designing that aims to fulfil public needs. He sees it as an index of modernisation and public service democracy in Britain's post-war pre-privatisation era: a large-scale unglamorous planning process open to rational justification, in contradistinction to 'the recent cult of the designer, who reveals expensive master-creations to a boardroom, as a *fait accompli*' (Kinross 1989, p. 52). Kinross refers to the fact that the design process in question involved a broadly composed committee, an outward look towards continental Europe,[72] assessment of relevant research, consultation with a large number of interest groups, a public debate, an expert designer, and technical advisers who conducted experimental research. Furthermore, the two committees and working parties in question were indeed not passive bodies. The minutes from the Anderson committee's 27 meetings and the Worboy committee's 19 meetings (and from numerous working party meetings) bear evidence of lively and constructive debates.

The dispute goes on. Factually unreliable accounts seem to be perpetuated, for example in a recent article on David Kindersley and his work by Robert Long, in the American typographic journal *Serif*:

> The all-caps alphabet that he designed used heavy, bracketed square serifs to promote legibility and intelligibility when seen from a rapidly moving vehicle. While it appears that practical tests *clearly demonstrated its superiority* to the Helvetica [sic] that was much in fashion at the time, Helvetica set in upper and lower case won (Long 1995, p. 35; my italics)

The same distortion applies to an illustrated web-page devoted to David Kindersley:

> Motserif – David Kindersley's capital alphabet for motorway signs. It *proved to be much more legible* than lower-case but less fashionable, and was not adopted (Typefaces by David Kindersley 1995; my italics).

Figure 15. Original sign layout and spacing template and the corresponding sign (advance direction sign for complex junction). 'Signs are laid out according to a system of preferred minimum dimensions expressed in stroke widths' (Kinneir 1968, p. [7]). 'The relative importance of each road is shown by differing the width of the route symbol' (Ministry of Transport 1963, p. 121).

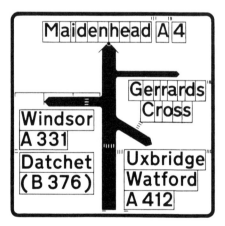 

A system design perspective

Designing in the twentieth century developed from small-scale crafting and planning of individual artefacts for mass production, to a situation in which whole systems are designed rather than individual artefacts. Kinneir's signing system is an interesting and early example of such 'system design', and with a graphic designer playing the central role. First, the sheer number of signs: a whole range of different kinds of traffic signs related to each other, with separate solutions for motorways, major roads and local roads. Second: all the practical considerations of layout, letterforms, size of letters, colour, background colour, reflection, illumination, mounting and siting, and not least, the content of the many different signs of each category. And third: the design of a system with prototypes and specifications which included a letter spacing system based on a limited number of tiles so the signs could 'design themselves', that is, so local sign manufacturers could easily space the letters consistently (or with 'tolerable uniformity'[73]) just by following the instructions in the manual (see figure 15). In fact, early on Kinneir explicitly regarded himself as a 'systemiser' and he was depicted thus in an article on 'the man you can't escape' in *The Sunday Times* in 1964:

> Kinneir sees himself primarily as a design 'systemiser', and it is perhaps his ability at taking organisational and financial considerations into account that so endears him to the official mind. (Hopkins 1964)

Epilogue

In 1994 the journalist Helen Fielding wrote a spirited account of British 'road sign madness' in the *Independent on Sunday*. She attacked the unsatisfactory situation on British local roads and streets, where signs are too often either lacking, or obscured, or in the wrong place, or cluttered together in such a way that 'motorists of Britain just don't know which way to turn'. She perceptively stated – and probably unwittingly echoed a modern usability engineering credo – that 'The trouble is, systems are usually set up by people who know the way anyway. They ought to be checked by people who are strangers to the area'.

More recently Phil Baines published a richly illustrated article on 'Kinneir, Calvert and the British road sign system' in the graphic design magazine *Eye*.[74] His article focuses on Kinneir's road sign system, but – like Fielding's – it also depicts a messy and unfortunate state of road direction signing in Britain today. Baines criticises clutter, lack of maintenance, poor application, the presence of pre-Worboys signs on many 'all-purpose' roads,[75] and the occasional use of non-standard letters. However, his criticism also extends to inconsistencies in a group of rather clumsy direction signs developed in the mid 1980s and formally prescribed in 1994.[76] These signs deviate markedly from Kinneir's principles.[77] They are map-type and stack-type direction signs where the pre-Worboys feature of boxes enclosing destination names has been re-introduced in the form of coloured panels behind the names. There is reason to believe that this solution – introduced with good intention but probably carried out without professional design advice – reflects a fundamental lack of understanding of the principles which underpin Kinneir's elegant and simple system.

73. PRO: MT 116/2, Working Party paper no. 42. See also MT 116/5: Committee Minutes 16, 18 Aug. 1963, which reveals that Kinneir wanted to develop a more foolproof system which would deal with imperfect spacing between certain letter combinations: 'It was *agreed* that the inherent imperfections demonstrated must be accepted on economic grounds.'

74. Baines, Phil. 1999. 'A design (to sign roads by): Kinneir, Calvert and the British road sign system'. *Eye*, no. 34, vol. 9, pp. 26–36. The article includes a section on 'Road signs in London' with photographs by Roman Inhoff and commentary by Nick Bell and Phil Baines, pp. 33–35.

75. The latest replacement date for pre-Worboys directional signs on all-purpose roads is now 1 January 2005 (Department of Transport 1994, p. 2). However, back in 1967 the Department proposed 31 December 1973 as the date 'for the completion of the traffic signs change-over programme' (*Sign World* 1967, p. 683).

76. These signs are described in Ball and Caddle 1989; Department of Transport 1991, pp. 16–17; Department of Transport 1994.

77. A similar criticism can be found in Kinross 1989.

78. The Transport Research Laboratory, in Berkshire, claims that it has no materials or documents from the legibility research that was carried out by the then Road Research Laboratory in the early 1960s; it further claims that there are 'no historical archives at all' at the laboratory (communication 8 February 2000 with Brian Cooper via Pat Baguley at the TRL). Neither the Departmental Record Office (of the Dept of the Environment, Transport and the Regions) in Hastings, nor the Motorway Archive at The Institution of Highways and Transportation, in London, have been consulted.

Acknowledgements

My thanks to Robin Kinross, Hyphen Press, London, for making me aware of some of the source material, and for his careful reading of an earlier draft of this article. I must also thank Margaret Calvert, Royal College of Art, who kindly gave me access to her collection of documents, and permission to cite letters written to or by Jock Kinneir. And not least, my gratitude to Paul Stiff for his encouragement and careful advice over a long period of time.

Thanks also to Phil Baines, Central Saint Martins College of Art and Design, who commented on a draft; to James Mosley who showed me the Kinneir/Calvert maquettes held in the collection of the St Bride Printing Library; to Paul Sturm at the Public Record Office; to Erik Hagen at Vegdirektoratet in Oslo (the Norwegian Ministry of Transport's Road Commission); and to Anthony Williams, of Harpenden, who provided me with several back issues of *Directions: newsletter of the Sign Design Society*.

An earlier version of this article appeared in my Reading doctoral thesis of 1999: 'Knowledge construction in typography: the case of legibility research and the legibility of sans serif typefaces'.

Archival sources

Minutes, notes, circulars, committee drafts, committee documents and correspondence cited, are either from files in the archives of the Public Record Office at Kew, or from the private collection of Margaret Calvert, London. Details are given in the notes. The following files at the Public Record Office (PRO) have been examined for this article: MT 116/1–17 (Traffic Signs Committee, 1961–1963); MT 126/1 (Motorway signs, 1955–1968); MT 95/28–29 (Street name-plates, 1947–1963).[78]

References

Bibliographical details about cited letters to the editors of newspapers, magazines and journals are given in the text or notes, and do not appear in the list below (see especially note 15).

ATypI. 1975. *Schriftenverzeichnis / Index of typefaces / Liste des caractères*. Introduction by Wolfgang Hartman. No place: Committee of Type Manufacturers of Association Typographique Internationale

Baines, Phil. 1999/2000. 'Letterforms surround us'. *Point: art and design research journal*, no. 8, pp. 5–13

Baines, Phil. 1999. 'A design (to sign roads by): Kinneir, Calvert and the British road sign system'. *Eye*, no. 34, vol. 9, pp. 26–36

Ball, Roger and Terry Caddle. 1989. 'The Guildford traffic signs project'. In the proceedings of the *Traffex 89 Conference: seminar on the future of traffic signs: 4 April 1989*

Bartram, Alan. 1978. *Street name lettering in the British Isles*. London: Lund Humphries / New York: Watson Guptill

Bauer, Friedrich. 1912. 'Schriften-Chronik'. *Klimsch Jahrbuch*, pp. 275–294

Bauer, Friedrich. 1928. *Chronik der Schriftgiessereien in Deutschland und den deutschsprachigen Nachbarländern*. 2nd edn. Offenbach am Main: Verlag des Vereins Deutscher Schriftgiessereien

Bernsen, Jens, Kai Christensen and Ib Møller. 1996. *Design af trafikkens skilte / Design of the Danish traffic signs*. Copenhagen: Danish Design Centre

Bertheau, Philipp. 1995. *Buchdruckschriften im 20. Jahrhundert: Atlas zur Geschichte der Schrift*. Ausgewählt und kommentiert von Philipp Bertheau unter Mitarbeit von Eva Hanebutt-Benz und Hans Reichardt. Foreword by Walter Wilkes. Darmstadt: Technische Hochschule Darmstadt

Burt, Cyril. 1959. *A psychological study of typography*. With an introduction by Stanley Morison. Cambridge: Cambridge University Press. (Reprinted in 1974 for the College of Librarianship, in Wales, by Bowker)

Burt, Cyril, W. F. Cooper, and J. L. Martin. 1955. 'A psychological study of typography'. *The British Journal of Statistical Psychology*, vol. 8, pt. 1, pp. 29–57

Charlesworth, George. 1984. *A history of British motorways*. London: Thomas Telford

Charlesworth, George. 1987. *A history of the Transport and Road Research Laboratory: 1933–1983*. Aldershot: Gower

Christie, A. W., and K. S. Rutley. 1961a. 'The relative effectiveness of some letter types designed for use on road traffic signs'. Department of Scientific and Industrial Research, Road Research Laboratory. Research Note no. RN/3931/AWC/KSR, January, 1961, not for publication

Christie, A. W., and K. S. Rutley. 1961b. 'Relative effectiveness of some letter types designed for use on road traffic signs'. *Roads and Road Construction*, no. 39, August, pp. 239–244

Christie, A. W., and K. S. Rutley. 1961c. '[Research] … on road signs'. *Design*, no. 152, August, pp. 59–60

Cohen, A. S. 1981. 'Car drivers' pattern of eye fixations on the road and in the laboratory'. *Perceptual and Motor Skills*, vol. 52, pp. 515–522

Crutchley, Brooke. 1980. *To be a printer*. London: The Bodley Head

Department of Transport. 1991. *The history of traffic signs*. London: Department of Transport, Traffic Signs Branch, Network Management and Driver Information Division. (Photocopied leaflet of 35 pages)

Department of Transport. 1994. *The design and use of directional informatory signs*. Local transport note, no. 1/94. London: HMSO

Department of Transport. 1995. *Know your traffic signs*. Fourth edition. London: HMSO. (1st edn 1975)

Design. 1959. 'Which signs for motorways'. No. 129, pp. 28–32

Die «klassische» Grotesk. Probe nr. 462. Berlin: H. Berthold AG (specimen of Akzidenz Grotesk; *c.* 1960)

Dreyfus, John. 1957. 'David Kindersley's contribution to street lettering'. *Penrose Annual*, vol. 51, pp. 38–41

Eason, Ron, and Sarah Rookledge. 1991. *Rookledge's international handbook of type designers: a biographical directory*. Edited by Phil Baines and Gordon Rookledge. Carshalton Beeches, Surrey: Sarema Press

Fielding, Helen. 1994. 'Life in the lost lane: motorists of Britain just don't know which way to turn: Helen Fielding on road sign madness'. *Independent on Sunday*, 2 October

Forbes, Colin. 1961. 'Comments'. *Design*, no. 152, p. 61 (one of three invited comments appended to Christie and Rutley 1961c)

Forbes, T. W., K. Moskowitz and G. Morgan. 1951. 'A comparision of lower-case and capital letters for highway signs'. In *Proceedings of the thirtieth annual meeting 1951*, vol. 30, pp. 355–373. Washington, DC: Highway Research Board, National Research Council (NB: all the publications that refer to this article, from around 1960 onwards, date it to 1950)

Froshaug, Anthony. 1963. 'Roadside traffic signs'. *Design*, no. 178, October, pp. 37–50 (republished in the volume *Typography & texts*, pp. 149–169, of the two-volume publication *Anthony Froshaug*, edited by Robin Kinross. London: Hyphen Press, 2000)

Handover, P. M. 1961. 'Letters without serifs'. *Motif*, no. 6, pp. 66–81

Harrison, Michael. 2000. 'Beyond the workshop'. In *ABCDavid Kindersley: a life in letters*, pp. 29–31. Cambridge: Kettle's Yard and Cardozo Kindersley

Hartley, James and Donald Rooum. 1983. 'Sir Cyril Burt and typography: a re-evaluation'. *British Journal of Psychology*, vol. 74, pt. 1, pp. 203–212

Hearnshaw, L. S. 1979. *Cyril Burt: psychologist*. London: Hodder and Stoughton

Hollis, Richard. 1994. *Graphic design: a consise history*. London: Thames & Hudson

Hopkins, John. 1964. 'The man you can't escape'. *The Sunday Times*, 13 December, p. 2

Hughes, Philip K. and Barry L. Cole. 1986. 'Can the conspicuity of objects be predicted from laboratory expertiments?'. *Ergonomics*, vol. 29, no. 9, pp. 1097–1111

Joynson, Robert B. 1989. *The Burt affair*. London: Routledge

Kindersley, David. 1960. 'Motorway sign lettering'. *Traffic Engineering & Control*, December, pp. 463–465

Kindersley, D. 1974. 'D. Kindersley'. In *Dossier A–Z 73*: Association Typographique Internationale, eds. F. Baudin and J. Dreyfus, pp. 73–74. Andenne: Rémy Magermans

Kinneir, Jock. 1968. 'Jock Kinneir'. *Dot Zero*, no. 5, pp. 5–11 (in a special issue devoted to the symposium 'Transportation graphics: where am I going? how do I get there?' held at The Museum of Modern Art, New York, 23 October 1967)

Kinneir, Jock. 1970. 'Det offentlige skilt'. In *Offentlig design*, eds. C. Ejlers, E. E. Fredriksen and N. Kryger, pp. 15–23. Copenhagen: Christian Ejlers Forlag (in Danish only)

Kinneir, Jock. 1971. 'Technical notes on the redesign of the United Kingdom road signs'. Unpublished manuscript, 15 + 7 pp; written for a Russian journal, but never published (Margaret Calvert, London)

Kinneir, Jock. 1980. *Words and buildings: the art and practice of public lettering*. London: Architectural Press

Kinneir, Jock. 1983. 'The ubiquitous alphabets of Jock Kinneir'. *Design and Art Direction*, July, pp. 18–21

Kinneir, Jock. 1984. 'The practical and graphic problems of road sign design'. In *Information design: the design and evaluation of signs and technical information*, eds. R. Easterby and H. Zwaga, pp. 341–358. Chichester: John Wiley

Kinneir, Jock. 1989. 'Worboys: 25 years on: a personal view'. In *Traffex '89 conference: the future of traffic signs*, 4 April 1989 (proceedings)

Kinross, Robin. 1984. 'Kinneir, Jock'. In *Contemporary designers*, edited by Ann Lee Morgan and Colin Naylor, p. 324. London: Macmillan Publishers

Kinross, Robin. 1989. 'Road signs: wrong turning?' *Blueprint*, October, pp. 50–51

Kinross, Robin. 1992. *Modern typography: an essay in critical history*. London: Hyphen Press

Kinross, Robin. 1994. 'Obituary: Richard Jock Kinneir'. *Directions: newsletter of the Sign Design Society*, vol. 1, no. 7, pp. [2–3]. (Extended and revised version of obituary first published in the *Guardian*, 30 August 1994)

Krampen, Martin. 1983. 'Icons of the road'. Special issue of *Semiotica*, vol. 43, nos. 1/2

Long, Robert. 1995. 'David Kindersley: in love with letters'. *Serif: the magazine of type & typography*, no. 3, 1995, pp. 32–37

Lund, Ole. 1999. 'Knowledge construction in typography: the case of legibility research and the legibility of sans serif typefaces'. Unpublished PhD thesis, Department of Typography & Graphic Communication, The University of Reading

Mackintosh, N. J. (ed.) 1995. *Cyril Burt: fraud or framed?* Oxford: Oxford University Press

Mason, John. 1994. 'British Airports Authority'. *Directions: newsletter of the Sign Design Society*, vol. 1, no. 6, pp. [1–3]

Mijksenaar, Paul. 1971. 'Typografie bij bewegwijzering'. *Graficus Revue*, no. 3, pp. 12–30

Ministry of Transport. 1962. *Traffic signs for motorways: final report of advisory committee*. London: Her Majesty's Stationery Office. (Title on the cover: *Motorway signs: final report of advisory committee on traffic signs for motorways*) (The report of the Anderson committee)

Ministry of Transport. 1963. *Report of the traffic signs committee: 18th April 1963*. London: Her Majesty's Stationery Office. (Title on the cover: *Traffic signs 1963: report of the committee on traffic signs for all-purpose roads*) (The report of the Worboys committee)

Ministry of Transport and Central Office of Information. 1965. *The new traffic signs*. [London]: Her Majesty's Stationery Office

Moore, R. L. n.d. [early 1970s]. 'The design of direction signs for road traffic: consultants report'. [Unpublished].

Moore, R. L. and A. W. Christie. 1960. 'Direction signs for motorways'. *The Engineer*, May 13, pp. 813–817

Moore, R. L. and A. W. Christie. 1963. 'Research on traffic signs'. In *Engineering for Traffic Conference*, pp. 113–122. London: Printerhall

Moriarty, Catherine. 2000. 'A backroom service? The Photographic Library of Industrial Design, 1945–1965'. *Journal of Design History*, vol. 13, no. 1, pp. 39–57

Morison, Stanley. 1996. *First principles of typography*. (new edition, introduction by Huib van Krimpen, preface by David McKitterick). Leiden: Academic Press Leiden

Mosley, James. 1964. 'Trajan revived'. *Alphabet: international annual of letterforms*, vol. 1, pp. 17–48

Mosley, James. 1999. *The nymph and the grot: the revival of the sans serif letter*. London: Friends of the St Bride Printing Library

Paterson, D. G. and M. A. Tinker. 1946. 'Readability of newspaper headlines printed in capitals and lower case'. *Journal of Applied Psychology*, vol. 30, pp. 161–168

Pedhazur, Elazar J., and L. P. Schmelkin. 1991. *Measurement, design, and analysis: an integrated approach*. Hillsdale, New Jersey: Lawrence Erlbaum Associates

Rainford, Paul. 1996. 'Motorway signs'. *Designing*, no. 44, summer, p. 13 (Wellesbourne, Warwickshire: Design and Technology Association)

Rooum, Donald. 1981. 'Cyril Burt's *A psychological study of typography*: a reappraisal'. *Typos: a journal of typography*, no. 4, pp. 37–40. (London College of Printing)

Schreiber, Hermann. 1961. *The history of roads: from amber route to motorway*. Translated by Stewart Thomson. London: Barrie and Rockliff

[Seemann, Albrecht]. 1926. *Handbuch der Schriftarten: eine Zusammenstellung der Schriften der Schriftgiessereien deutscher Zunge nach Gattungen geordnet*. Leipzig: Albrecht Seemann Verlag

Shaw, Montague. 1989. *David Kindersley: his work and workshop*. Cambridge: Cardozo Kindersley Editions and Uitgeverij de Buitenkant

Sign World. 1967. Vol. 2, no. 10, November–December. (Special 'Road traffic signs issue')

Smith, Allen. 1998. *Motorway archive: Chapter 1: History: up to the Special Roads Act 1949 – leading to the construction of the Preston by pass 1958*. London: The Institution of Civil Engineers and the Institution of Highways and Transportation (unpublished)

Souttar, James. 1992. 'The voice of the establishment'. The Monotype conference 1992, Cambridge, 1–3 September

Spencer, Herbert. 1961. 'Mile-a-minute typography?' *Typographica*, new series, no. 4, pp. 2–28

Spencer, Herbert. 1961. 'Comments'. *Design*, no. 152, p. 61 (one of three invited comments appended to Christie and Rutley 1961c)

Statens Vegvesen. 1987. *Skiltmaler: tekniske bestemmelser og retnings-linjer for offentlige trafikkskilt, vegoppmerking og trafikksignal*. Oslo: Statens Vegvesen

Stephenson, Kerry. 1971. 'Jock Kinneir has designs on signs for the times'. *Building Design*, 8 January 1971, no. 42, pp. 6–7

Stone, Reynolds. 1961. 'Comments'. *Design*, no. 152, p. 61 (one of three invited comments appended to Christie and Rutley 1961c)

The Times. 1958. 'Road signs 2ft. high: designs for new motorways: legible at 70 m.p.h.', 2 December 1958

Typefaces by David Kindersley. 29 October 1995. http://www.icce.rug.nl/erikjan/bluefuzz/David-Kindersley/node4.html#SECTIO (9 April 2000)

Call for typography papers

Typography papers welcomes new papers on typography and graphic communication, and also papers at the meeting places between typography and other disciplines.

Please send three paper copies of your typescript, double-spaced and with wide margins. On acceptance, subject to refereeing, we will ask you to supply the text of your paper as a word-processed file.

Send proposals or papers to:
The editor, *Typography papers*
Department of Typography & Graphic Communication
The University of Reading
PO box 239, Reading RG6 6AU
England

fax 0118 935 1680 (international +44 118 935 1680)
e-mail p.stiff@reading.ac.uk